Who You?
Hawaii Issei

Dennis M. Ogawa
and
Christine Kitano

Japanese Cultural Center of Hawai'i
Honolulu, Hawai'i

Library of Congress Cataloging-in-Publication Data

Names: Ogawa, Dennis M., author. | Kitano, Christine, author.
Title: Who you? Hawaii issei / Dennis M. Ogawa and Christine Kitano.
Other titles: Hawaii issei
Description: Honolulu, Hawaii : Japanese Cultural Center of Hawaii, [2018]
Identifiers: LCCN 2018007521 | ISBN 9780824877286 (pbk. ; alk. paper)
Subjects: LCSH: Japanese—Hawaii—Biography. | Japanese
Americans—Hawaii—Biography. | Plantation workers—Hawaii—Biography.
Classification: LCC DU624.7.J3 O3725 2018 | DDC 996.9/00495600922—dc23
LC record available at https://lccn.loc.gov/2018007521

This publication is printed on acid-free paper
and meets the guidelines for permanence and durability
of the Council of Library Resources.

Cover photos courtesy of the Hawaii Times Photo Archives Foundation

Printer-ready files provided by the authors.

Distributed by
University of Hawai‘i Press
2840 Kolowalu Street
Honolulu, Hawai‘i 96822
www.uhpress.hawaii.edu

For
Matsuo "Matsy" Takabuki

Contents

	Acknowledgments	ix
	Preface	xi
1	**Masaji Marumoto**	1
	Tamajiro's Hawaiian, Japanese, and American Outlook	
2	**Sparky Matsunaga**	21
	Issei: A Life Beyond Logical Answers	
3	**Patsy Sumie Saiki**	29
	Hawaii Interned: The Spirit of Family, Ohana, and Aloha	
4	**George Ariyoshi**	49
	Father and Mother: Otagai and Seeing the Bright Side	
5	**Fumiko Kaya**	61
	The Legacy of Katsu Goto: Helping Others	
6	**Fujio Matsuda**	71
	Human and Family Values Unite Us	
	Epilogue	77

Afterword   79
The World of the Issei in the 1930's:
A Photographic Glimpse by Kaoru "Kay" Ueda, PhD,
Curator of the Japanese Diaspora Collection,
Hoover Institution Library and Archives,
Stanford University

Appendix   95
Key Resources on the Issei

Acknowledgments

In 1868, 149 individuals from Japan arrived in Hawaii. We call them the Gannenmono, or First Year Men, because their arrival coincided with the first year of Emperor Meiji's reign. While most returned to Japan within 3 years, about 50 men remained and chose to make Hawaii their home. In recognition for the Gannenmono's decision to "cast their lot" together with the people of Hawaii, King Kalakaua asked the highest officials in Japan to send more Japanese to the islands. The Gannenmono served as a testament of the goodwill between the two countries. They opened the door for future Japanese to leave the mother country and come to Hawaii.

These 50 individuals are the true pioneers and original Issei. We see the influence of the Gannenmono everywhere—from the integration of Japanese into Pidgin English and the prevalence of plate lunches to the highest levels where a single state plays a unique and substantial role in maintaining U.S.-Japan relations—it is clear that the Gannenmono's decision to live and work together with the people of the islands has shaped the Hawaii we know today.

As we celebrate the 150th anniversary of the arrival of the Japanese in Hawaii it is our hope that this book contributes to honor the Gannenmono and all those who chose to cast their lot together with the people of Hawaii.

Preface

If a Hawaii Issei were to ask, in their local Japanese English, "Who you?", the answer would begin and end in a story. Stories express identity, and for Hawaii Japanese Americans, these stories are all about the Issei, the founding generation. It is because of their stories that Hawaii Japanese Americans often say, *Okage sama de*: "We are who we are because of you. We are deeply obligated." Many do not forget that they are who they are thanks to the fortitude, will, and venturous spirit of the Issei.

The first group of Issei arrived in Hawaii in 1868. This group is known as Gannenmono, or, "first year men," because they arrived in Honolulu in the first year of the reign of Emperor Meiji. This was a small group of about 149 laborers. After three years working in the sugar plantations, most returned to Japan. Some went onto the mainland. About fifty remained. These Gannenmono were truly the first Issei. For the Hawaiian Monarch, King Kalakaua, they would become the living testament of the positive feeling he had for the Japanese. They were individuals who chose to work, who chose to stay and who chose to cast their lot together with the people of Hawaii. He recognized and expressed openly to the highest officials in Japan his desire to have more Japanese come to the islands.

Because of his efforts, many Issei came to Hawaii between 1885–1924. Most were young, healthy male laborers who wanted to earn money to send back to their families. But conditions proved to be difficult working on the island sugar plantations. Of about 180,000 who came between 1885 and 1924, the majority returned to Japan.

The stories here are about the Issei who chose to stay in Hawaii. They numbered about 39,000. Though fraught with challenges, it was ultimately a decision they would not regret. Issei life was difficult— Japanese immigrants faced anti-Japanese sentiments, unfair racial practices, and harsh working conditions. However, instead of viewing themselves as sojourners or temporary workers who must simply endure such hardship, they envisioned themselves, like the Gannen-mono before them, as individuals who would cast their lot together with the people of Hawaii and build a better future for families and succeeding generations. Instead of bowing to the pressures of planta-tion life and unjust treatment, they took a dedicated, long-term view of their chances in Hawaii.

Many did not stay on the sugar plantation. In 1900, over 70 percent of the plantation workers were Japanese but by the 1930's only about 20 percent were Japanese. Some Issei became fishermen. Others raised Kona Coffee. A few were hired by rich white families and became domestic servants and gardeners. With the help of friends and the practice of tanomoshi, or mutual lending, certain individuals were able to open stores or start a business. All worked hard and maintained a frugal way of living.

From 1907–1923, wives and picture brides traveled across the Pacific Ocean to meet their husbands on a new shore. They started families, and by 1915, 46% of the babies born in Hawaii were of Japanese ancestry. That birth rate rose to more than 51% in 1923, which is to say, every other baby born in the islands was Japanese. The growth of families provided a stabilizing influence, and the Issei community began to flourish. The 1930's saw the rise of Japa-nese language schools, religious institutions, stores, markets, farms, restaurants, and social and professional organizations. Enterprising Issei built successful small businesses. Additionally, leisure activities, such as baseball and fishing, or reconnecting to the arts and music of Japan, became a part of the Issei experience. The world of friendship and sense of community expanded and grew. Issei family businesses, husbands, wives and children, served the diverse needs of Hawaii's multi-ethnic and inter-racial communities. Customers became friends and long term relationships were established. Japanese, Chinese, Filipino, Hawaiian and Haole families enjoyed attending community sports and leisure events together.

The emerging Issei community became an integral part of Hawaii's make up. For the Issei, though they ceased living in Japan, they never ceased being Japanese. They loved Japan and they loved Hawaii, too. To love Japan did not require the exclusion of their love for Hawaii, or vice versa. The Issei were proud of their unique identities as Hawaii Japanese Americans because Hawaii, with the community they had built, was their home. The Issei would never hesitate to tell their children, "Lucky Come Hawaii."

The stories in this book are based on the personal reflections of the descendants of the Issei. They provide a glimpse of the Issei, their character and outlook. The stories unite us all in honoring the memories of ancestors who ventured to new worlds with the universal hope of making a better life for their families. The stories help to answer the question: Who you?

Who You? Hawaii Issei

Masaji Marumoto

Tamajiro's Hawaiian, Japanese, and American Outlook

When Masaji Marumoto died in early 1995, the combined Sunday edition of the two major Honolulu newspapers published an article, "Marumoto often was first, and foremost," reporting on the passing of a man who had ranked first in McKinley High School's storied 1924 graduating class, who was the first of Asian ancestry to graduate from Harvard Law School, the first Asian American president of the Hawaii Bar Association, and when Hawaii became a State, the first Asian American to serve as an associate justice on the Hawaii Supreme Court—or, it could have been added, any American appellate court of highest jurisdiction. He was the only Japanese American to serve in the U.S Army's Judge Advocate General Corps during World War II.

In 1985, Masaji Marumoto received an honorary doctorate degree from the University of Hawaii. He was also a historian and wrote definitive essays on Japanese immigrants and the Hawaiian government. In one essay, Marumoto documented in detail that the Hawaiian government originally wanted Japanese immigrants not merely for economic reasons, but to help replenish the native Hawaiian population.

The first group of Japanese laborers arrived in Honolulu on June 19, 1868, on the British ship, *Scioto*. The *Scioto* took 34 days to cross the Pacific. As Marumoto notes, one of its passengers, Yoneki-chi Sakuma, kept a brief diary of the voyage. "The first three days in the open sea were stormy, and not a soul had a meal. The days after the storm were long and monotonous…."

The *Scioto* docked with 149 souls aboard: the group leader, or headman, 141 male workers, six women and one infant. They were known as Gannenmono, or "First Year Men," "Meiji one." After their 3-year contract expired, 89 men chose to stay with about 40 moving to the mainland. Many of the remaining males married Hawaiian women, and melted and merged into the stream of native life.

Through this experience, Hawaiian officials held firmly to the view that the Japanese were desirable, not only as laborers, but as a repopulating element. This view was most clearly expressed by John M. Kapana, who King Kalakaua appointed on September 23, 1882 as envoy extraordinary and minister plenipotentiary to Japan. At a dinner he gave in Tokyo honoring three imperial princes and the nation's department heads, Kapana stated:

> His Majesty [Kalakaua] believes that the Japanese and Hawaiians spring from one cognate race and this enhances his love for you. He hopes that our people will more and more be brought closer together in common brotherhood. Hawaii holds out her loving hand and heart to Japan and desires that Your People may come and cast in their lots with ours and repeople our Island Home.

In his essay, Marumoto concludes by making an observation of an event that took place one hundred years later:

> The Aloha Week celebration held on October 20–26, 1968 in Honolulu provided a dramatic sequel to the merging of Gannen-mono into the Hawaiian society. The festival king was James Kaanapu, a swarthy, handsome young man, as Hawaiian-looking

as any person can be, a natural to play the monarch in a Hawaiian festival. Neither the media nor the celebrants noticed that he was the great-grandson of Sakuma, the immigrant who kept the diary of the *Scioto* voyage.

What Marumoto reveals in this essay represents only a small part of the research he would undertake and the stories he told so well. Masaji Marumoto contributed greatly to the knowledge and documentation of the first-generation Japanese in Hawaii.

No matter how impressive his achievements were, however, Masaji Marumoto never wanted to talk about himself. In all the interviews and oral histories conducted with him, Marumoto would primarily devote himself to stories centered on his Issei father, Tamajiro.

For Masaji, his father exemplified what the Issei generation was all about—remarkable immigrants totally committed to a future in Hawaii. They were individuals who made Hawaii their home; their children would be American of Japanese ancestry.

Masaji Marumoto was most happy to provide this account of the Issei, his father, Tamajiro Marumoto.

Masaji Marumoto

"Tamajiro's Hawaiian, Japanese, and American Outlook"

I was born on January 27, 1906, in Honolulu, the third child of Tamajiro and Matsu Marumoto to survive infancy. Two brothers born in 1902 and 1910 died at six months and one month.

Since my mother died when I was only four years old, the most influential person in my upbringing was my father, Tamajiro Marumoto. He was born in 1863 in the village of Okimura on the small island of Nomi in Hiroshima Prefecture. He came to Hawai'i as a government contract laborer when he was twenty-five years old. Between 1885 and 1894, 29,069 Japanese immigrants came to Hawai'i. The vast majority of these were contract laborers for the sugar plantations, but they also included women, children, and male domestics. They came on twenty-six shiploads. My father came with the sixth group, aboard the *Takasago Maru*, arriving in Honolulu on November 14, 1888. As with all contract laborers, my father was issued a *bango*--a number stamped on a metal tag for identification of a people whose names were entirely foreign and unpronounceable to management. On the ship's passenger list, my father is listed as contract laborer number 5,140, which was his *bango*.

My father was from a poor farming family but had gone to school in Japan for the mandatory four years of primary education. He had an excellent command of written and spoken Japanese. Coming to Hawai'i at age twenty-five to work on a sugar plantation was a bold decision for a man of his age, who was also the eldest of eight children. I think that to leave the land of his birth to seek new opportunities in Hawai'i, my father must have possessed a wonderful spirit of adventure.

On November 18, 1888, my father was contracted out to Pā'auhau Plantation, on the Hāmākua coast of the Big Island of Hawai'i. In those days there was no good road from Hilo to Pā'auhau or to a harbor in Hāmākua, so ships would anchor right below the sheer cliffs near Pā'auhau. The ships had booms operated like primitive ski lifts and winched the laborers to shore on seats.

My father began with the customary three-year contract and renewed it for another three, so he worked on the plantation for a total of six years. For working ten hours a day, twenty-six days a month, he earned $15.00 a month. From that small sum, deductions were taken to pay off his travel expenses from Japan and as compulsory savings to be deposited with the Japanese Consulate. His take-home pay was $8.65 per month, from which he had to buy his food.

In 1895, after his six years on the plantation, my father came to Honolulu and worked at the S. Shimamoto Store, a Japanese store on the edge of Chinatown. In August 1899 he went back to Japan to marry Matsu Nakayama, the young woman his father had selected for him. Born in 1881, my mother was only eighteen when she married my father, who was thirty-six.

After five months in Japan, as my father was preparing to return to Hawai'i with his now pregnant wife, he received a letter from Mr. Shimamoto saying that the store had been destroyed in the great Chinatown fire of January 20, 1900, and asking that he return as soon as possible to help in rebuilding it. My father was uncertain about the state of the bubonic plague, which the fire had been set to combat, and did not want to expose his wife and child to it, so he returned to Honolulu alone in May 1900. It was a full year later that my mother and eldest sister, Tamako, born in July 1900, arrived in Honolulu. Having been born in Japan, Tamako was a Japanese subject and remained ineligible for naturalization until the passage of the Walter-McCarran Act of 1952.

The Shimamoto Store was rebuilt on Merchant and Alakea, where First Hawaiian Bank now stands. My father worked at the store another seven years while living in Kaka'ako, where my sister Chiyoko was born in 1903 and I in 1906.

In 1907 a man originally from my father's village in Hiroshima had a store in Captain Cook, Kona, on the Big Island, which he wanted to sell so that he could go back to Japan. He offered the store to my father for $700. My father bought it sight unseen. So when I was a year and a half, my parents, two sisters, and I sailed to the Big Island, where my father became a Kona merchant and coffee farmer for the rest of his life. The T. Marumoto General Store was located on two acres of leasehold land of the Henriques estate, a well-known Portuguese landowner there. In 1929 my father built the Kona Theatre next to the store. The front of the store was at road level, but the land behind it sloped down steeply, which allowed for sleeping quarters and a warehouse under the back part of the store.

Kona was a remote place, not easily accessible. The only contact Kona had with Honolulu was by ship that came once every ten days. There were a number of men who escaped from their plantation labor contracts and came to Kona because they knew chances of being pursued by their employers were slim. They would assume aliases, and only when they sent for picture brides and needed to show their family record would their real names become known.

My oldest sister Tamako, seven years old when we moved, didn't like Kona and wanted to go back to Kaka'ako to attend school. So my father sent her to board with the Masashi Masuda family. Mr. Masuda was the founder and principle of the Kaka'ako Japanese Language School.

In 1910, when I was four, my mother died. Two months before she died, she had given birth to her fifth child, another son Tokio, who lived only a month. My mother was illiterate when she married my father, but over the years he had taught her to read and write, and she had gotten to the point where she could write simple letters to her family in Japan. About the time her newborn son died, my mother received word that her favorite younger brother in Japan had also died. My father always felt that those deaths were two great blows to her health.

There was little medical care available in the Kona area. My mother succumbed to what was probably childbed fever. The only memory I have of her was watching her in the store taking cans down from the shelves, wiping off the tops, and putting them back. If not for a few photographs, I wouldn't remember what she looked like.

My father was a man of few words but he was devoted to his children. He tried to meet my needs, as his only son and youngest child without a mother around. Although I had been born with a clubfoot, that didn't stop me from wanting to play baseball with the other boys. They had been playing with bats they made from branches. My father bought me gloves and a bat to share with the boys so they would let me play with them.

Despite being allowed in on baseball games, I think I was an introvert growing up because I was born crippled and couldn't participate in sports much. Besides the clubfoot, I broke my other foot when my donkey threw me off. I didn't tell my father, thinking that I couldn't have gotten medical treatment for it anyway. So I ended up with two deformed feet.

After my mother's death, Chiyoko also went to live in Honolulu, to be with Tamako at the Japanese School in Kaka'ako. Chiyoko was a bright, spunky kid. She often won the egg-in-a-spoon race and told me the trick was to watch the egg, not the finish line.

From then on I saw my sisters only when they returned to Kona for summer vacation. When it was time for them to go back to Honolulu, my father would take me with him to see them off on the interisland steamship anchored in Kailua Bay. Since the water was too shallow for the steamers to anchor at the wharf, passengers had to be ferried on a whaleboat to the ship, which also carried cattle. But first they had to wait for the cattle to be swum out to the ship and loaded. In those days, cattle seemed to be more important than people. On Chiyoko's first trip to Honolulu, she kicked up such a fuss, refusing to leave, that my father handed me over to a neighbor to take me back to Captain Cook, and he jumped on the boat to take his daughters to Honolulu.

When I was about five, my father brought me on a business

(Left to right) Chiyoko, Tamako, Tamajiro, and
Marumoto at age 5, 1911.

trip to Honolulu and took me to Kakaʻako where I had been born.
As we approached a house in the area, he pressed a silver dollar into
my hand and said, "Masaji, you're now going to see the woman who
brought you into this world. When you see her, give this dollar to
her." As we walked up to the house, a plump Hawaiian woman came
running out and started hugging and kissing me. That was the first
kiss I remember ever getting. She was the midwife who had attended
my birth.

That evening my father left me at the Masuda's home with my
sisters. Because there wasn't enough room for him there, my father
went to stay with his Honolulu wholesaler, Masao Kawahara, whose
home was across the street from Queen's Hospital where the Department of Education building is now. After my father left, I began

crying and wouldn't stop. Finally at midnight Mr. Masuda had to order a horse-drawn hack to take me to the Kawaharas' because I wouldn't sleep and just cried for my father.

I vividly remember another, sadder journey to Honolulu. Early one afternoon in April 1912 a wire came to Kona that Chiyoko was seriously ill. She had been playing barefoot on the unpaved streets of Kakaʻako and had gotten a *keʻawe* thorn in her toe, and the wound became infected with tetanus. There were no tetanus shots in those days. Later, about 5 o'clock, another wire came saying that she had died. Chiyoko was eight years old. To get to her funeral in Honolulu, my father wrapped me in a blanket and drove a horse and buggy through the night and morning from Kona to Kamuela, where we had lunch at a friend's home. Then we traveled a couple more hours to the harbor at Kawaihae and caught a ship for the twelve-hour voyage to Honolulu. Since Chiyoko was right above me in age, I missed her for a long time after she died.

The supplies for the Marumoto Store came primarily from Hackfeld, which later became American Factors. Its main branch was in Kailua, but the one that supplied our store was in Nāpōʻopoʻo. The manager there was Portuguese. My father spoke only rudimentary English but his Hawaiian was fluent, and I remember he spoke only Hawaiian with the Portuguese manager. If the Nāpōʻopoʻo branch didn't have what my father needed, he would go to the Kailua branch, an all-day affair by horse and buggy, taking me with him.

My father didn't send me to school until I was seven because it was two and a half miles away. Because of my clubfoot, he felt I wasn't strong enough at age six to walk that distance. Later he gave me a donkey to ride to school. I would tie the donkey to a tree in the graveyard of the Buddhist temple and go to Japanese and English schools.

Japanese School, conducted by the Buddhist temple, Kona Hongwanji, was across the road from the English school, Konawaena School. Japanese School started at 7 in the morning. At 9 the

Konawaena principal would ring the bell and the Japanese School students would run across the road. Classes at Konawaena were held from 9 to 2, with a short period for lunch—for the Japanese students it was usually rice balls and dried fish from home. Every Friday after lunch, the students spent an hour cutting grass with sickles kept by the school.

At night my father would carry me downstairs to our sleeping quarters. We got up about 5 in the morning. Our water came from a large wooden tank that caught rainwater. After washing up, my father and I would sit before the Buddhist altar and chant sutras. A half hour later, we would take a lamp and pail and walk to the Greenwell Ranch to get fresh milk.

Besides the store, my father had a drayage business with more than a dozen horses and mules for hauling coffee and felled *koa* and bringing freight up from the Nāpōʻopoʻo wharf. There was one employee whose sole chore was to cut fodder for the horses and mules. The fodder grew on land that my father leased about a mile away. This fellow, a bachelor who lived near us, made pancakes on a wood-burning stove and let me flip them. They were plain hotcakes, the batter sweetened only with sugar, for butter and syrup were too expensive. So every morning after getting the milk, I would go to this kindly worker's house, eat the pancakes I flipped, and go back home to pick up the lunch my father prepared, and go to school.

Although I started first grade late, after that I spent only a few months in second grade and caught up by third grade. I went to Konawaena School through the sixth grade. Many students ended their schooling at that point in order to help their parents in the coffee fields. Anyone who went through the sophomore year of high school was considered very educated. Few graduated from high school.

In 1916, when I was ten, my father remarried and took my stepmother, my sister Tamako, and me to Japan for the dedication of several large gifts he had made to his home village. Because he had not earlier taken care of his parents, when he had accumulated some savings, he sent money to the village to build a beautiful entry gate to its Buddhist temple and a building to store Buddhist scriptures and also to buy a set of scriptures, all in memory of his parents.

After the dedication, he gave a big party at the family home. There the priests of the temple said to my father, "I suppose you're eventually going to send your son to a university in Tokyo?" My father replied, "No, I'm going to raise my son as an American."

Later my father told me, "I have fulfilled my obligations to my parents and to my village in Japan, so I don't have to go back." That was his last trip to the country of his birth. He had made Hawai'i his home.

It was when we came back to Hawai'i that my father told me to expatriate. I was only ten years old.

And yet he never forgot his home village. I found out after my father died that in 1939, shortly before we took him on a trip to the

Dedication of Tamajiro's gifts to his village—entry gate to
the Buddhist temple and a building for scriptures, 1916.

mainland, he donated a burial plot for the soldiers from his village who had died in the war going on in China. He had the plot built with concrete posts and steel rods all around—it was beautiful. But during World War II, the Japanese army needed so much steel that they took all the steel rods away and left only the concrete posts standing. I saw it some years later when I went to Japan, and I said I cannot leave it this way when my father, for love of his village, donated it. So I asked my cousin to get an estimate of the cost to restore it to its original condition. He wrote me the amount and said that instead of steel rods, they would install chains from post to post. I sent the money and they made it the beautiful burial plot it had been. And the village sent me a medal.

When I was in sixth grade, there were about ten students in that grade, six in seventh grade, and two in eighth grade. One teacher taught the three grades. At the time, World War I was raging in Europe. While the teacher taught one grade, he had the other two grades knit socks and sweaters for the soldiers overseas.

Kona was a community where everyone spoke Japanese, and I felt I wasn't learning enough. I wanted to get out. I said to my father, "Send me to Honolulu." I wanted to go to Mills School, a boarding school, which later became Mid-Pacific Institute. My father agreed, but when I came to Honolulu and stayed temporarily at Masao Kawahara's home, Mr. Kawahara told me, "Don't go to Mills because you'll lose touch with the Japanese language. Stay with us and go to public school and Japanese School."

Mr. Kawahara and his family were now living deep in Kalihi Valley where he owned 30 acres, most of it an orange grove. Besides a large family home, he provided boarding facilities for sons of his neighbor island customers so that they could get higher education in Honolulu. During the six years I boarded at the Kawahara home, I attended both English public school and Japanese language school, and I worked at his store, M. Kawahara Shoten, after school and on Saturdays. The Kawahara store occupied two buildings, still standing, at the corner of Maunakea Street and Nimitz Highway, across from Honolulu Harbor.

Japanese School, conducted by the Hongwanji Mission, started at 7 in the morning, so we boys would leave Kalihi Valley about 5:30 on a jitney bus to downtown, then walk to the Buddhist temple on Fort Street—now Pali Highway—for our Japanese classes.

In those days, admission to the English public schools was dependent on fluency in English, and I had difficulty getting in because of my poor English. The nearest school was Royal School, but that place was always filled up. One of the better schools was Central Grammar School, which later became Central Intermediate School. When I went to apply there, the principal, Mrs. Overend, asked me, "What grade are you going to be in?" Country kid that I was, not speaking good English, I was scared. "Seventh grade," I said. She said, "Fourth graders in my school speak better English than you," and sent me away.

The only English school that would accept me was the grammar school of Normal School. There the elementary students served as guinea pigs for the high school students, called cadets, who were learning to be teachers. In the first year, Normal School cadets just learned the fundamentals, but from the second year, the sophomore year, they started teaching under supervision. Upon graduation, they became teachers. They were not required to have a college degree.

I attended seventh and eighth grades at Normal School. Then I went to McKinley High School. My English was still so poor, my first grade in English at McKinley was a C-minus. I almost flunked out. But by the end of that first year, I pulled my English grade up to a B-plus.

McKinley was then the only public high school on Oʻahu. The curriculum was very demanding. We had four years of English, four years of math, and three years of Latin. We also had general science and biology, ancient and medieval history, American history, sociology, and economics.

I had excellent teachers at McKinley. The one who had the most influence on me was Esther Thomas of Omaha, who taught at McKinley only one or two years. She was the one who first asked me if I wanted to go to college. I said I did but wasn't sure I could. She did very well in getting this Asian student, whose home language was Japanese, to become interested in Shelley, Keats, Byron, and Alexander Pope. She encouraged me with poetry such as Pope's: "A little learning is a dangerous thing; / Drink deep, or taste not the Pierian spring; / There shallow draughts intoxicate the brain, / And drinking largely sobers us again." That was pretty heady stuff for a Kona boy.

In 1922, when I was fifteen, just before my sixteenth birthday, I arranged to renounce my Japanese citizenship. At that time descendants of Japanese subjects born in Hawai'i held dual citizenship. They were Japanese citizens by blood and American citizens by birth. There was a provision in Japanese law for expatriation, but one had to expatriate before age sixteen. As he had since I was ten, my father urged me to expatriate.

Expatriation was simple. The problem was establishing American birth with witness testimony. There was no compulsory law to register one's birth when I was born, so I had to get a certificate of Hawaiian birth from the secretary of the Territory. I went on my own to the secretary's office to make the necessary arrangements, but I had an awful time getting the certificate because of my witnesses. The woman who knew about my birth was so timid, she couldn't give her testimony correctly. She got confused. She said she wasn't in Honolulu when I was born. Another witness who was supposed to know about my birth told me, "What do you want to become an American citizen for? Japanese citizenship is enough for you." However, I finally got my birth certificate.

I prepared my own petition for expatriation and filed it at the Japanese Consulate. When it was granted, I notified the office in my father's home village and my name was crossed off as a Japanese subject. For my father, my expatriation meant that he would be the last of his family as his family record was wiped out, but he had wanted me to take this step. I was one of the few to expatriate Japanese citizenship that early.

At the end of my high school junior year, when I went home for summer vacation, my father asked me what I wanted to do after graduation. I told him I wanted to go to college. The early 1920s had been poor years for both coffee and his store. He told me that the only way I could attend college would be if I worked my way through. Of course, in those days, that was usually the case.

I graduated in the famous McKinley High School class of 1924. Among the class of 237 students I graduated first in the class and was awarded a gold medal.

I applied to the University of Chicago because my father wanted me to go where I knew someone. Dr. Isamu Tashiro, the son of a plantation worker from the same village as my father, had graduated from Chicago Dental College and was practicing dentistry there. During my junior year at McKinley, Doc had come to Hawai'i to visit his family. I met him and remembered him as a very friendly, outgoing person. So when I applied to Chicago, it was essentially to be near this family friend. I did not know of the university's standing, that it was as good as I found it to be.

I was fortunate. I received a scholarship from the Prince Fushimi Scholarship Society of Japan. The Fushimi scholarship paid for my transportation and $600 a year for four years. With this financial aid, and with the sense of adventure my father had when he sailed from Japan to a new world so many years before, I left Hawai'i looking forward to my new life as a college student on the mainland.

The journey by ship and rail from Hawai'i to Chicago was an unforgettable first-time adventure for a boy who had grown up in Kona and Honolulu.

When I finally arrived in Chicago, it was too late to get a room in the dormitories, which were all filled, so I had to go to a rooming house near the university where I rented a room for about ten dollars a month.

The only other Hawai'i student on campus was Robert Murakami, who was studying law. Little did I know that we would later become law partners. Bob was about five years older than I and very helpful to me.

I took only two courses during my first quarter, I took four courses the next term. After that, I regularly took four courses each quarter and went to summer session, so at the end of my second year, I had finished my third or junior, year. I chose philosophy as my major because I had had a wonderful philosophy professor during my first year. He was originally from Texas and had a great sense of humor. Although I didn't really know what philosophy was when I began college, he was such an inspiring teacher that I started to take more and more philosophy courses.

When I wrote to my father that I was majoring in philosophy, he raised hell with me. He wrote back, "Why don't you take something practical?" To please him, I shifted over to economics because I also enjoyed the courses I took from Professor Jacob Viner, a leading economist of the time who later taught at Princeton. Although I now had a more "practical" major, I continued with philosophy as my minor.

At Chicago, to be elected to Phi Beta Kappa required an A-minus average for three years or a B-plus average for four years. I completed my junior-year courses by the end of my second summer and had averaged better than A-minus, so I was elected to Phi Beta Kappa at the end of that second summer.

Although the University of Chicago offered me a fellowship in economics, I felt that there was little future in that field for persons of Asian ancestry. I knew a couple of young Japanese men from Hawai'i who had graduated in economics on the mainland who couldn't find jobs. I therefore decided to go to Harvard to study law.

When I made that decision, I had never been in a lawyer's office or even a courthouse, either in Hawai'i or in Chicago.

I completed my third year at Harvard and received my law degree in 1930. I returned immediately to Kona, staying with my father until the bar examination that October in Honolulu.

The Hawai'i bar exam was actually a fairly recent institution. Previously, law graduates applied for a license from the supreme court by petition. I was the fifth person of Japanese ancestry to be licensed to practice law in Hawai'i.

After working at various law firms in Honolulu I opened my own office in August 1932. It was located on the second floor of the biggest Japanese bank in Hawai'i, Yokohama Specie Bank, at the corner of Merchant and Bethel.

In 1937 I expanded my law practice when I formed a partnership with Robert Murakami, my former schoolmate from the University of Chicago.

Two years later, in 1939, I finally decided to take a vacation. I had been a lawyer for eight years and been married for six, but I had never taken my father or my wife on a trip. I decided to go to either Japan or the mainland. I asked my father, "Which way do you want to go?" He said, "I don't want to go to Japan. I want to see the mainland." And of all the places on the mainland, his greatest wish was to see Washington, D.C.

In August 1939 we embarked on the *Empress of Canada* to Vancouver. From there we went to Seattle, where we stayed with one of my Harvard classmates, took a train through the Canadian Rockies, and continued on to Chicago, and then Detroit where we bought a car, a blue Mercury, to drive the rest of our trip. We drove through eastern Canada and down to Boston where we saw Harvard and stayed with another Harvard classmate.

We then spent two weeks in New York, going to the World's Fair among other sights and activities. My father had a wonderful time, for there he got into the habit of getting up early in the morn-

Marumoto, Shigeko, and Tamajiro in Canada, 1939.

ing and doing his own exploring. As he walked, he would draw a map of the streets he traversed.

On our last night in New York, my father said with a smile to Shigeko, my wife, "I've seen all I want to see." She thought, "For heaven's sakes," she later told me. She tried to explain to him that we were only halfway through our trip, we still had to drive back across the country, and there would be lots to see.

He said quietly, "There's nothing more to see."

We thought he was just tired. In retrospect, I think he was deeply content; he felt his life was complete.

The next day we drove from New York to Washington. The following day, Saturday, September 30, my father, as had become his routine, got up early in the morning and went on an outing of his own. We waited for him to come back, but he didn't. Worried, I checked with the police and all the hospitals—nothing. We waited, with growing anxiety, and I checked again. It was then that a police officer said,

Marumoto and Tamajiro at the New York World's Fair, 1939.

"There's a Chinese man about fifty years old in the Emergency Hospital. He was hit by a streetcar around 9 this morning."

I instinctively knew that was my father. Shigeko and I went to the hospital and found him in a coma. My father was unconscious for five days before he died on October 5. In his pocket was a map he had sketched, showing the streets he walked from the hotel to the exact spot where he was struck. Apparently the streetcar had stopped, and he stepped off the curb as it started up again.

At the time of the accident, my father was a robust seventy-five years old and in perfect health. Because he was a staunch Buddhist,

I asked a Buddhist minister to come down from New York to per-
form the funeral ceremony. My Harvard Law School classmates
working in Washington were the pallbearers. We had my father cre-
mated, and we carried his urn as we drove back across the continent
and sailed home. So he completed his journey with us.

Shigeko and I returned to the Islands in mourning.

Sparky Matsunaga

Issei: A Life Beyond Logical Answers

The Issei came from a land rich with folklore and supernatural beliefs. When they came to Hawaii, they brought with them a multitude of myths and superstitions.

For the Issei, the supernatural, good or evil, was a real force in their life, a dimension of their ethnic and religious identities. Spirits and communications with the dead were part of many Issei experiences. It was also the case, in the early plantation camps of Hawaii, for Chinese, Filipinos, Puerto Ricans, Koreans, Portuguese and all the Hawaiians. The ability to talk to the dead, to employ supernatural powers, was institutionalized in most of the immigrant communities. For the Issei, specific men or women, called *odaisan* or *kōbō-daishi*, were recognized as being clairvoyant or capable of healing illnesses by invoking the power of the spirits. These *odaisan* were highly respected in the immigrant community and served as spiritual comforters to the suffering and bereaved. You have a strange skin disease which doctors diagnose as untreatable—the *odaisan* blesses, heals. Your daughter is bothered by visions of a male ghost—the *odaisan* wards off the evil, gives protection. Your mother has died, but her spirit is restlessly reappearing—the *odaisan* slips into a trance, speaks to the dead. You want to know about the future—the *odaisan* has visions, divine omens. Especially in the small rural Japanese communities, the *odaisan* became supernatural "brokers." Imploring the spirits of the dead, satisfying the needs and fears of the living, their role was indispensable.

In several cases, the *odaisan* would also be required to exorcize the spirit of demons who had possessed the soul of a living human being. In Japan, forms of possession were usually described as being caused by one of several animal spirits—the fox, cat, badger, or snake. One such animal spirit which the immigrant transported to Hawaii was the *inu-gami,* or dog spirit. Barking like a dog, running about on all fours, attempting to commit violence, the person bewitched by the *inu-gami* would terrify the village, evoking ancient fears of witchcraft.

A startling account of possession by the *inu-gami* and subsequent exorcism by an Issei healer is described by the late Senator Sparky Matsunaga. The events are seen through the eyes of Senator Matsunaga as a young boy growing up on Kauai.

Imploring the spirits to drive the evilness out of frantic victims, Matsunaga's father challenged the dog spirit with a mixture of Buddhist prayer and fundamental Japanese folk beliefs. In this story, Matsunaga tells us of two experiences of witnessing his Issei father's power to cure a person possessed by the demon entity.

Sparky Matsunaga, raised in Hanapepe, Kauai, graduated from Harvard Law School and went on to be a highly respected and popular politician, elected in 1962 to the U.S. House of Representatives and in 1976 to the U.S. Senate. He was loved by his Hawaii constituency. Elders would say, "I no grumble about Uncle Sam no more…Sparky now in Washington."

For both Democrat and Republican sectors, Matsunaga was noted for his hard work, legislative skills, and wisdom. He was a member of key congressional committees and, given his expertise, co-authored the book, *Rulemakers of the House.*

Though a master of legal documentation and factual directives,

Sparky Matsunaga hosting Hawaii's Cherry Blossom Queen,
Amy Fukuda, in 1969 on a tour of the Capital.
His highest priority was service to his constituency.

Sparky Matsunaga did not hesitate to tell us here, in this story, that he was the son of an *ikibotoke,* an individual who could communicate with a demon spirit. His Issei father was a living saint who played a vital role—he was the balancing force between the supernatural and the real.

For Matsunaga, there is more to life than logical answers.

Issei: A Life Beyond Logical Answers

Inu-gami no sawarimono, or illness caused by the dog spirit, used to be very prevalent on the island of Kauai in the late 1930s and immediately preceding World War II. There were individuals in Japan, particularly from the Hiroshima prefecture, who had the power to use the spirit of the dog to bring about illnesses in others, a power inherited from generation to generation within a family. Whenever a person who had the power of the dog spirit wanted someone or something which a person possessed very badly, then he would set a curse and the person would fall ill. The victims of the *inu-gami* would become weak, and would be unable to eat or sleep, and would finally just waste away.

As an *ikibotoke*, or living saint, my father was recognized on Kauai as sort of a spiritual healer. He healed people of all kinds of

Sparky Matsunaga with his parents, Kingoro and Chiyono Matsunaga.

illnesses. And one of the illnesses that my father was capable of curing, and one which doctors could do nothing about, was the illness of the *inu-gami*. One of my father's most frightening experiences, and one which I witnessed, was the case of a Mr. I____ who was possessed of this evil spirit. He came to my father and asked if anything could be done to cure him. My father took him to the temple, had him kneel before him and then started praying. My father must have prayed for almost an hour or more, hypnotically chanting: "*Namu–Myōhō–renge–kyō, Namu–Myōhō–renge–kyō, Namu–Myōhō–renge–kyō.*" As my father chanted, he swayed the *gohei*, or the pom-pom-looking instrument which he used in praying, over the head of the victim, touching him from shoulder to shoulder.

Suddenly, Mr. I___ got up on all fours and started barking like a dog, running out of the temple onto the highway. Others who had been present at the ceremony ran after him until he fainted from exhaustion. They carried him back to the temple where my father said a few words waving the *gohei* over Mr. I___. And Mr. I___ opened his eyes, cured of his illness.

A second case which happened about 1937 involved a classmate of mine. Soon after high school graduation, she married and eventually gave birth to a baby boy. One morning, shortly after giving birth, she suddenly grabbed a butcher knife and, with an insane stare in her eyes, was about to the slay the boy. When her husband tried to stop her, and took the baby away, she started chasing the husband with the butcher knife. The police were called, who finally subdued her. Since this incident happened in Hanapepe, Kauai, the police wanted to take her to the sanitarium at Kaneohe on the island of Oahu, the *pupule* house. But the parents of the young victim begged the police to permit them to take her to Mr. Matsunaga, the healer, to see whether he could cure her. So, with handcuffs on they brought her over to my father's temple. As soon as she saw my father, though, she cowered away, as if dreadfully afraid. My father commanded her, the victim, to approach him. And she obeyed as if she were a little puppy, turning her head away from him, but then gradually obeying the command to approach him. My father ordered her to kneel before him over the Japanese *goza* or straw mat, covered by a *zabuton*, a little Japanese cushion. Then my father turned to the altar to pray, and he prayed and prayed and prayed, "*Namu-Myōhō-renge-kyō*," waving the *gohei*. Here again the prayer must have lasted about an hour.

Then my father stopped and asked the girl, "Who are you?" "*Omae wa dare ka?*" "Who are you?" as if he were talking to an unknown person. Now in most cases of those who are inflicted with the spirit of the dead, the victim speaks almost as if a ghost from the past; the voice is the voice of the dead. Relatives who have been sitting nearby, witnessing the scene, have later testified that the victim would speak not with their own voice, but the voice of the spirit of the dead person who happened to be in the victim. This young lady responded to my father in a voice not her own, "You know who I am. I don't need to tell you who I am. You know who I am." Of course, my father knew who used the dog spirit, but would never relate it to others. He however confided to my mother who warned us against close association with certain families who lived on the island of Kauai.

After the young girl spoke to my father, she sprang up on all fours and started barking like a dog and whining. She ran out of the temple onto the yard and towards the highway, trying to elude my father. Her husband, her brother and my brother-in-law chased after her and she must have gone about a hundred yards on all fours until she dropped from exhaustion and fainted. Upon the instructions of my father, she was carried back into the temple where he waved the *gohei* and said a few words. She suddenly opened her eyes, looked up and said, "Where am I? How did I get here?" She was cured.

The police officer who had accompanied her to the temple was amazed. After questioning her, the girl appeared absolutely sane, so he turned her over to her husband and her parents. For years afterwards this cured victim of the dog spirit visited my father's temple, giving thanks almost on a daily basis.

The stories which I have related seem impossible, almost incredible to believe. I perhaps would not have believed them myself if they had been told to me by others. But I have actually witnessed with my own eyes these happenings. As an educated man, I have tried to rationally and scientifically understand these strange occurrences, to look for reasonable explanations. But without logical answers, I am inclined to believe, at this time, that there is something more to life, something more than what the sciences have been able to explain. There is an entity called spirit, whether it be good or evil—a spirit with which some of us can communicate. And I am convinced that my father was one of those blessed with the supernatural powers to perceive things one step beyond the rest of us.

{ 3 }

Patsy Sumie Saiki

Hawaii Interned: The Spirit of Family, Ohana, and Aloha

The war period (1941–1945) dramatically altered the course of the Japanese American experience. Both in Hawaii and on the mainland, Japanese Americans feared what the future might hold. How would a population of alien Issei and their children fare in a nation at full war with Japan?

On the mainland, war resulted in the wholesale incarceration of an ethnic group. Over 110,000 Japanese Americans, of whom one-third were Issei, were removed from California, Oregon, Washington, and portions of Arizona. In Hawaii, because Japanese Americans constituted a major percentage of the population and were a vital labor force for the island's defense economy, mass removal was not instituted. However, the government did seek to contain the Hawaiian Japanese American community by incarcerating approximately 1,320 revered elders. The Issei community leaders were picked up within hours of the bombing of Pearl Harbor on December 7, 1941. Hawaii's Japanese Americans were stripped of their bishops, priests, school teachers and principals, respected business executives, and heads of community organizations—the spiritual, cultural, educational, and business leaders. These individuals represented the heart and soul of Hawaii's Japanese American community.

29

When we talk about the Japanese American concentration camp experience, stories must be told about the "wrong committed" and the forces and people responsible—a time when America's notion of justice failed and racism prevailed. Such stories must not be forgotten. They challenge us to not allow such violation of democratic ideals to happen again. There are other stories still of the camps that deserve recognition. Patsy Sumie Saiki, a gifted writer, presents stories of the Hawaii Issei imprisoned for nearly four years in detention sites located primarily on the mainland. Patsy Saiki recounts for us how these leaders endured the harsh conditions in these camps. In addition to reading diaries and other documents in both English and Japanese, Saiki interviewed over 100 internees to record their experiences. Because of her conscientious work, we gain a close perspective of how the internees remained composed and patient in the face of such injustice.

Patsy Sumie Saiki

As Saiki highlights, the internees rose above what was beyond their control and maintained their spirit of aloha; their hope to return "home" to their beloved families in Hawaii sustained them, as did their camaraderie and commitment to their fellow inmates. Kumaji Furuya is one of the major voices in Saiki's stories. Like other incarcerated Hawaiian Issei, Furuya held leadership positions in the Japanese community. He was head of the Honolulu Japanese Chamber of Commerce and played a key role as Vice President in the largest Japanese organization in the islands, the Honolulu United Japanese Society. Both organizations were broadly characterized as "pro-Japanese." Furuya was arrested at his house on the afternoon of December 7, 1941, and was subsequently taken to a number of camps over a span of four years. The camps included Camp Livingston in Louisiana, Camp Missoula in Montana, and Camp Forrest in Tennessee.

As part of the record of his life in the camps, he would compose haiku:

Livingston
> Baggage hanging over our
> shoulders We trudge toward
> summer clouds

Missoula
> Life has become routine
> Men spend their time polishing stones

Camp Forrest
> At night
> Imprisoned in a faraway
> place I hear the cicadas sing

Furuya also composed this short song:

Moon Over the Camp

    Leaving green islands to travel thousands of miles
    Across oceans and mountains
    We arrive in America, far, far, north,
    The land buried in snow.

    Surrounded by high barbed wire,
    Without even a penny,
    A summer hat in the snow,
    Canadian winds penetrate my soul.

    A bright moon, a clear evening sky
    Thinking of my beloved family
    Left behind in a faraway place
    Who knows my aching heart?

    Yet, when I think of the thousands in the world
    Suffering more than I
    The snow on my shoes feels lighter
    As I wait for peace to return.

In the above poems, Furuya makes clear the suffering endured by the internees. The juxtaposition of his imprisonment and the song of the cicadas conveys his sense of deep isolation. Similarly, in the song, Furuya speaks to the heartache of being away from his "beloved family." And yet, Furuya still finds perspective in his situation. In the song's final stanza, he acknowledges that there are many in the world who suffer. This thought gives him, not comfort, but patience for "peace to return." Such lines demonstrate the Issei character and spirit we honor in these stories*.

Hawaii Interned: The Spirit of Family, Ohana and Aloha

Sand Island, Hawaii

After his imprisonment at the Immigration Station in Honolulu following the bombing of Pearl Harbor, Furuya and the other inmates were moved to Sand Island, Hawaii. The men spent day after day wondering when they were going to be released, when the military would finally decide they were innocent of any disloyal act to the United States. Some were allowed to leave Sand Island.

Each day Kumaji Furuya waited to be called to the Hearing Board at the Immigration office. Would it be today? Would he be able to meet his family tonight? Finally, at long last, his name was called.

Furuya gave his friends whatever he had that could be of some use: his soap, his handkerchief, his undershirt. In turn he was given messages to give to his friends' families, although the urgency was now missing, since soon all or almost all of them would be released.

Furuya was taken, again by barge, to the docks which were camouflaged and protected with machine guns. The luxury liner *Lurline* was painted a dark grey over its formerly gleaming white; instead of tourists, it now took families of military men back to the Mainland. The piers were barricaded. Despite all this, Furuya felt free and he took deep breaths of ocean air. Then, as they neared the pier, he saw some young men stacking boxes. One looked so much

---

* The haiku and the short song are from Suikei Furuya, *An Internment Odyssey: Haisho Tenten* (Honolulu: Japanese Cultural Center of Hawaii, 2017), Livingston, 123; Missoula, 164; Camp Forest, 97; Moon, 278.

like his son, his heart thumped. Could it be? But then the youth turned; it was a Chinese boy.

He reported again to the Immigration Office interrogators. The examiner asked, "What is your occupation?"

"Owner, furniture store." Strange, for them to be asking more questions when they were about to release him.

"Who do you think will win this war? Which side do you want to win? Why did the Japanese bomb Pearl Harbor without declaration of war? Who gave Japan information regarding ships at Pearl Harbor? Why did you go to Japan three years ago? How much money did you donate to Japanese organizations last year? How much English education do you have?"

The next day was New Year's Eve. When Furuya's name was called, he was overjoyed. He might be able to spend New Year's Eve with his family....

Instead, he was issued a number: ISN-HJ-CI 188!

When he reported back to Sand Island with an embarrassed smile and joke, someone returned his soap, another his undershirt, a third his handkerchief. It would be four years before Furuya would be allowed to return home to his family.

Camp Livingston, Louisiana

Uncertainty and insecurity had plagued the Hawai'i internees as they moved from camp to camp. In December, 1941, it had been the Immigration Station in Honolulu. Then had followed Sand Island in January, Angel Island in San Francisco in February, Camp McCoy in Wisconsin in March, Fort Sill in Oklahoma and Camp Forrest in Tennessee in May, and now Livingston, Louisiana in June, 1942.

As they walked from the train station to the Livingston camp in the 100-degree weather, staggering not only from the heat but from the heavy duffel bags they were carrying, they were allowed to rest without the threat of being shot. Also, the guards treated them with consideration, and when soldiers from some barracks they were passing tried to take pictures of the stumbling group, the guards yelled out a warning. One soldier who persisted had his camera confiscated. When the internees saw this, they passed the word down the line, "This is going to be a humane camp, a good camp."

Some of the new arrivals staggered into camp bent under the weight of their suitcases. They had been told the suitcases would be brought by truck later, but many would not trust the suitcases out of their sight, since these had once disappeared for three months. They quickly revived when they saw a sign which read, "ALOHA." It brought tears to see this word again, this word which symbolized their beloved Hawai'i.

Camp Livingston already had over 700 internees: 400 from the West Coast states, 160 from Panama and Costa Rica, and 166 from Hawai'i. The 180 new arrivals were alphabetically divided into groups and placed in barracks numbered J1 through J4. The West Coast's 400 Japanese were in K1 through K4. The J barracks also included the Central Americans, and Furuya was in J1 which was comprised chiefly of Panamanians.

While at Camp Livingston, the internees planned and organized different activities to keep themselves alert and physically well.

A Rev. Kano from Grand Island, Nebraska, started a botany-farming class. He had few enrollees at first, as no one wanted to be out in the heat. But when he started taking students outside the barbed wire fences into cool gullies, he gained an overflow class that had to be divided into two sections.

In the gullies, the men encountered eels almost two feet long which slithered in the wet rocks and slimy grass. These reminded the Hawai'i men of snakes; the internees were as afraid of eels as they were of snakes. They also saw armadillos for the first time, and spiders identified as poisonous.

They found other objects in the pine groves. One was a six-inch oval rock, often lying on the paths they used. When they kicked it aside, they found it had several pairs of legs. This was the land turtle, whose tiny babies could fit on one's thumbnail.

Another pine grove object was the snake. There were several varieties. The Peruvians taught the Hawai'i men which were poisonous and which were not, but the Hawaiians could never learn. They feared all snakes—every color, every size, moving or still, dead or alive. But the Peruvians merely stamped on the snake's head, even poisonous ones, slit the snake lengthwise, and pulled the skin off in one swift movement. They used the skin to make belts or purses, and ate the snakes broiled.

Furuya, on one of his field trips, found a stone hollowed out with another stone in it. It sounded like a rattle, and brought back memories of when his son, Robert, was a baby. At night, Furuya would rattle the stone before going to sleep, and when he forgot, someone would murmur, "Furuya forgot his rattle."

As the days grew colder the men also held classes. Some men offered English, Japanese, and Spanish classes. Others taught classes in wood-carving, painting, calligraphy, business, geography, history, philosophy, and *shakuhachi*, Japan's unique flute-like instrument. Each man shared his talent.

Some of the other men decided to put on a play. Producing a play was easier said than done. First the group had to beg, borrow or steal pots, pans and other objects that could produce sound—this would be their band. Itsuo Hamada, from Maui, wrote a play. Costumes had to be devised, and many a window curtain and pillowcase were sacrificed. Music was written and rehearsed. Makeup was improvised, including wigs for women's roles from dyed potato sack fibers. The Panamanians went into the mountains to cut wood for the benches. This required cutting down a tree, splicing the trunk to make bench-size slats, sanding the wood to eliminate splinters, and cutting and sanding other pieces of wood to make "horses" for the slats.

The play was a big success financially, for each person donated a dime to see the play. More important, there was a special feeling of closeness among the camp members involved in the play. A decision was made that night: let's have another play within four months.

In this feeling of camaraderie, there was a sudden chill. The Panamanians could be seen whispering among themselves, but would stop when a Hawai'i internee walked by. Finally, one of the Central Americans approached Furuya, since he lived in their barrack.

"Mr. Furuya, you know the benches we made for the play?"

"Sure. It's in the dining room."

"That's the problem. It's not. Some of the Hawai'i men have taken the benches and are using them for shelves and bookcases. We think it's unfair of them to use the benches as private property."

"I'm sorry. I didn't know that."

"Well, maybe the first person thought taking one bench would be OK. But someone else took another one, and so on, and now, when we put on the next play, we'll have a hard time getting the benches back because the people would be accustomed to them. They would consider it their private property by that time."

"Let me see what I can do," Mr. Furuya promised.

It was only a few weeks later that Mr. Ogata from Hawai'i needed an operation for ulcers. But the hospital had no blood plasma. Would any of the over 300 men from Hawai'i be willing to be tested and donate blood if necessary?

Most of the Hawai'i men were elderly so they were fearful. The food was not too nutritious, they said, and they were not healthy. Could Furuya ask the Panamanians instead?

Furuya hesitated. It was only a few weeks since they had been resentful about the "borrowed" benches. How would they feel about the Hawai'i men now asking them for a favor? But it was Mr. Ogata's life that was at stake, so Furuya approached the leader of the Panamanians to ask if his men would be willing to help Mr. Ogata by going for a blood test and then donating blood if it was needed. "Sure." Six of them volunteered unhesitatingly and immediately. Furuya wept. He was so proud of being with the Panamanians.

Fort Missoula, Montana

Fort Missoula turned out to be a military reservation which had once housed Indians. Always, it seemed, they were sent to Indian reservation outskirts. There was the usual messhall, laundry and showers, but this one had a real theater.

To the southwest was a mountain range. To the east were battlefields where, it is said, the Bitterroot River which ran next to it ran red with blood during the Indian wars. Now there was fish in the clear cold water which flowed from the mountains which were still covered with snow. Wild flowers carpeted the fields, and there were even some purple iris bordering the barracks planted by someone who had lived there earlier. It was a quiet, beautiful place.

The commander, P.H. Fraser, gave them self-rule and each block elected a mayor, vice-mayor, secretary and treasurer. To Furuya's surprise and delight, most of those elected were from Hawai'i. He was pleased that Hawai'i internees had earned so much respect from the others.

Also, at Missoula, each man regained his own identity. In the days following Pearl Harbor, Furuya had been identified as ISN-HJ-CI 188. For so many months, he had been an impersonal number, like a convict. Well, why not? He had been incarcerated just like a convict.

But now he regained his name and address: Kumaji Furuya, Box 1539, Honolulu, T.H., U.S.A. He felt like a human being again.

Within each dormitory—no longer called barracks—there were 38 to 40 people. Every ten dormitories of about 360 men had their own messhall, showers and latrines. The men cleaned their own dorms, heated the bathwater, and helped with messhall responsibilities. Beyond that, they were free to engage in camp activities.

When the group was settled, the younger men again wanted a golf course, so they got hoe, rake, pick and shovel and constructed a 9-hole course. When the grass grew, the course was almost as beautiful as that at Oʻahu Country Club, which did not admit Japanese as members but which they could see from certain parts of Nuʻuanu.

It was getting close to December, so some of the men were given passes to shop in town; a single guard accompanied them, indicating trust. The trees along the mountain roads leading to town were scarlet and gold, and in Missoula itself, a town of about 18,500, willow trees draped green branches over the street, casting a lacy shadow over curbs. It was an indescribably romantic town.

Furuya was surprised at the merchandise in the Missoula Mercantile Store, for he found food, drugs, cosmetics, farm equipment, clothing, sporting goods, recreational supplies and even padded blankets, resembling the futon at home. On the walls were heads of reindeer, wolf, buffalo and other animals, with a plaque to indicate who the hunter had been.

Furuya bought some material and other items to be sent as gifts to his family in Honolulu. The salesgirl asked, "Are you Mexican?"

Here it comes, thought Furuya. "No, I'm Japanese."

"Japanese? Do you live in town?"

"No, we live in a camp a few miles from here. It's an internment center."

"What's that?"

"That's where they keep some of the aliens of those countries against whom the U.S. is fighting this war. Countries like Germany, Italy, Japan…"

"Are you from Japan?"

"No, I'm from Hawaiʻi."

"But Hawaiʻi is not our enemy, is it? Why do Japanese from Hawaiʻi have to be in an internment camp?"

"That's what we'd like to know," Furuya smiled. His heart was full, as he inwardly blessed her. How wonderful it was, to be treated as just another human being, not an individual tainted with disloyalty.

As the autumn days passed, even the crows began disappearing. One misty twilight, the men saw a sight they had never seen before.

The sky above them was black with ducks that cawed their way south.

The next morning those who woke up early and went outside found some ducks had crashed into buildings. Others had been injured, caught on wires. A minister found one, and called it manna from Heaven. They all had duck for dinner that night, but the meat was tough and stringy, unlike their chickens.

The winter chill came early and suddenly. The apple growers in the surrounding area, caught by surprise, asked the camp commander if some of the internees would be willing to help pick apples. The men realized it would be tiring work, but at least it would be something different, so some volunteered. The men left early in the trucks provided, and picked the dark pink, firm and juicy apples all day.

"How come we never see this type of apple in Hawai'i," they asked.

"These bruise easily. And if they're bruised they spoil within a day or two, so they're not good export apples," they were told.

When they returned to camp, they were allowed one paper sack of free apples. A sack held about eight apples. But each man had more than eight friends, and he wanted all of them to taste these apples. So each worker tightened the leggings on the pants, buttoned shirt sleeves and shirt, and filled the space next to the body with apples. Ballooned, they stood like robots or clowns all the way home, for they couldn't sit. But what joy there was at camp, as they distributed an apple to as many men as possible.

The colors and coolness of autumn was soon replaced by frigid winter weather. Some of the men caught cold and were hospitalized for days or weeks. They looked pale and wan, like Japan tourists who used to come to Hawai'i in late February or March. Furuya himself went to the hospital a few days before Christmas and thought he was getting better when, on New Year's Eve, a Catholic priest came and prayed over him. Now why did the priest do that? Were these the "last rites" he had read about in books? Was he dying and no one was brave enough to tell him? "Tell me the truth," he insisted, but his friends said the hospital wouldn't give them any information regarding patients.

Then an orderly brought *mochi, nishime,* and *sushi* on New Year's Day. The Japanese food tasted so good, he knew he couldn't be dying. A dying man would not have had such an appetite. He secretly poured his medicine into a potted plant and soon became well enough to return to the dormitory. Because it was cold—32 degrees on January 17, and several degrees below zero at night— the others brought his food from the dining room back to the barrack.

It was soon after New Year's Day that the camp received such items as tea, soy sauce, *miso* and Japanese medicine, sent by the Japan Relief Fund through the Red Cross. 50,000 pounds of tea, 8,600 barrels of soy sauce, and 500 tons of books in the Japanese language were delivered to internees in both WRA and Department of Justice camps.

"I guess we're Japanese after all," the men said. "Even when we're in a camp and Japan is at war and losing, at that, still the Japanese people sacrificed this food for us. To them we are fellow Japanese, and they want to comfort those of us in internment camps." That night they sang *Kimigayo,* the Japanese national anthem, to thank the Japanese people for their sacrifice and thoughtfulness.

But the internees' respect for Americans grew too. One spring day, some of the men were allowed to shop in Missoula. When the purchases had been completed, the men wandered off to a cemetery close by and strolled casually through the grounds glancing at moss-encrusted tombs. Suddenly someone called out, "Look, look! How did a Japanese get here?"

"A Japanese? Buried here? Why, here's another!"

"And here's one…"

In all, they counted 50 graves of Japanese. They had died between 1900 and 1909, about 30 to 40 years ago. Some had emigrated from Hokkaido and Niigata in northern Japan; others had come from warmer Hiroshima and Wakayama. One had been only 18 when he died, another 19. The majority had been in their 20s and 30s, and a few had been from 59 to 63. The name of the person, his date of birth and death, and his *ken*—his province—identified the man buried under each tombstone.

Had they come before the turn of the century to work on the railroads? Why had the 18-year-old and 19-year-old died? Had they not been able to adjust, coming from warm Hiroshima, to work in cold and rugged Montana? What had Montana been like, in the first decade of the 1900s? Had they starved to death? Got caught in an epidemic? Froze during a cold winter? Had the survivors been able to get word to parents in Japan as to what had happened to their beloved sons? Why had so many died in a period of only nine years? Who had provided for these tombs? Was the last Japanese to die also buried here?

The site of their graves was clean. Someone had mowed the grass, cleared the weeds, and even scrubbed the mold from the tombstone.

Later, 24 priests received permission from the camp commander to hold Buddhist services for the deceased. They burned incense at each grave. Their tears fell, not for the young men who had died without having their dreams realized, but in gratefulness that the town residents had cared for the graves for so many years, and especially now, knowing the ethnic origin of those buried below.

"Those leaders who interned us are Americans," the priests said. "But these Missoula residents are Americans too. These Americans are thoughtful enough to care for graves of unknown people. At home, in Hawai'i, some children neglect to clean around their own parents' gravesite. And here are Americans who have kept these Japanese tombstones clean."

"Yes, the Americans are people with consideration for other

human beings. They are human beings first, not Americans or Japanese first."

The cold winter was less cold after that discovery.

Camp Forrest, Tennessee

The first U.S. Pacific War prisoner was Ensign Kazuo Sakamaki. He was the skipper of a midget submarine which malfunctioned and washed ashore on Oʻahu the day of Pearl Harbor.

Sakamaki would be imprisoned with the Hawaiʻi internees. One day at Camp Forrest he began to talk with Furuya:

"Ah, you have a Japanese face and name, and you use the Japanese language, but inside you're no longer Japanese. You have a different philosophy. For example, we in Japan don't feel much responsibility for others, although we're taught to fight and die for our country. But then country—the term country—is an ideal, a nebulous idea. We're trained from an early age to believe that our country comes first—before ourselves, before our families. We must be able to sacrifice ourselves and our families for our country. But that way we're not relating to individual people, to our friends, our neighbors…people who have names and faces and sorrows and joyful experiences and worries. The country comes first, and within it are these people…But another way of looking at it is, these people are precious, these people are worth fighting for…and these people constitute our country. It's like looking from two ends of the same kaleidoscope. I think that's what makes this country, America, great. You care for each other. I see you sharing your sad moments, your happy moments. You almost live each other's lives…"

"Well," Furuya said, "There's so few of us, and nothing else to do. We have to listen to others and even to our own conscience. We now have the time and opportunity to evaluate our past and our values, our expectations, our goals in life, our relationships with others."

"You have the Japanese in you, but you also have the American…"

"Perhaps it's the Hawaiian influence, more than the American influence," Furuya mused. "In Hawai'i there's something that's called *ohana* or extended family. That's a larger family relationship where members care and share with each other. The fish they catch, the taro they raise, the weaving of the *lauhala* for floor mats, the wood for fire, the fruits and vegetables they raise cooperatively, all these they share…maybe not equally, but according to the amount of work put in. It's similar to our *kenjinkai*, except that it's a more tight-knit group."

"*Ohana?* In Japanese it means a flower! That relationship—of caring and sharing—is as beautiful as a flower."

"And do you know that in old Hawai'i, and even today to some extent, the Hawaiians have what is called a 'calabash' cousin? I used to hear the Hawaiians say, 'So and so is my calabash cousin,' and I would ask, 'On your father's side or your mother's side?' and they would answer, 'Neither! He's a calabash cousin…'"

"What's a calabash cousin?"

"A calabash is a big round gourd cut in half, dried, and used as a container. Well, when there's a birth, marriage, emergency such as fire or flood, or death in a family, people gather to help. Whoever comes drops an offering into the calabash, without a name identifying who gave how much. Can you imagine? There's no way the receiver can know how much the giver gave. You see, the giver gives from his heart, and according to what he can share or wants to give to the new couple or bereaved family. That is a true friend or a calabash cousin!"

"Then there's no way to know who gave $1 or who gave $50?"

"Yes. And it doesn't matter to the giver because he's giving, not to be acknowledged for his gift, but because he wants to share in that happy or sad occasion. In Japan…and in Hawai'i…we put our money in envelopes with our name and address on the outside."

"Calabash cousin!" Sakamaki said softly. Then he added, "Furuya-san, may I be your calabash cousin?"

Furuya began assessing the Hawai'i internees with greater awareness. Did they really care and share the way Sakamaki said? He thought of Masayuki Chikuma, who was always joking, chanting legends and reciting folklore to while away the time. He was so positive in his actions and conversations. Yet he was mischievous enough to make sake from rice, wine from raisins and over-ripe fruit, and thoughtful enough to share these odd-tasting concoctions with different groups in the barracks.

Then there was Otojiro Ozaki, the teacher from Hilo. Ozaki was the philosopher-poet, taking a specific incident and relating it to the whole of life. Ozaki was that rare individual who could detach Ozaki the poet from Ozaki the man and view life from a different plane, like a circling eagle observing the vast 180-degree world below and around him, and at the same time noticing a tiny mouse scurrying in the open fields. He could see the vast forest, but he would also be aware of the fuzz on the under-side of a new tree leaf.

There was Katsukichi Kida, the nephew of Sutematsu Kida, the sampan skipper killed on the morning of December 8, 1941 as he was returning from a fishing trip. During the winter, Katsukichi would make many trips from the dining hall to the barracks to bring food for the aged and the ill, so they could remain in their warm beds. He would clean around their buildings, and even sweep the snow off the roof, although he had once slid from the roof to ground with a broom still in his hand. When others asked, "Kida-san..." he never had a prior commitment, a sore back, a cold, or a headache. "Hai!" he would promise and he always kept his promise.

Sakamaki was right, Furuya acknowledged.

The Return

At the camps, no matter how difficult or unfair life seemed to be, one could exist if one had friends. Furuya, Ozaki, and Chikuma had numerous friends. The secret, if there was a secret, was in caring and sharing—caring for one another and sharing both the good and the bad. That was such a hackneyed, or over-used statement! Priests and ministers had been preaching that for ages, but now, finally, the internees realized this was true.

How trite—caring and sharing. They were sophisticated international businessmen. They associated with leaders of two countries. Most of them were wealthy enough to be independent. And yet, it was true. Caring and sharing—one's relationship with another, the ties with others—the family, the neighbors, friends, other businessmen, why, this was the most important and rewarding aspect of life!

"You remember when we attended Makiki Christian Church? By the time I shook the pastor's hand at the door, I had forgotten the sermon. Yet, 30 or 40 years later, I can see in my mind's eye Rev. Okumura talking about love and relationship. Caring for others and sharing joys and griefs—the way we are doing in this camp—is this what the old-time Hawaiians called 'calabash cousin' relationship?" Furuya mused.

Throughout the four years the men were called by many labels: prisoners, detainees, internees, disloyals, renunciants, alien enemy, enemy aliens, Jap! But usually the labels described the person using it. Lt. Col. Rogers of Camp McCoy had called them "gentlemen" because he himself was a gentleman, a quiet and compassionate human being. There were those who categorized and stereotyped the internees as "disloyal" even before any individual had evidenced disloyalty. These were the persons trained to expect disloyalty, and any move by any Japanese was cause for suspicion. On the other hand, Robert L. Shivers, the FBI special agent in Hawai'i, had looked for and expected loyalty, and he had received it.

Whether branded "loyal" or "disloyal," it had been a long and tiring four years. But finally, in October, 1945, two months after the atom bombing of Japan and the end of the war, the internees received word the camp would be closed toward the end of the year.

Furuya returned to Honolulu on November 13, 1945, after an absence of four years. *Left to right:* Hanzo, Seizo, Albert Tomochi, Robert Keiichi, Furuya, Florence Yoko, and Jun. *Courtesy of the Japanese Cultural Center of Hawaii.*

When the men returned "home," they knew in what country that was. The crowd that cheered them at the pier, the words ALOHA and WELCOME HOME held high over the crowd, the *leis*, the gifts, the tears, the love.

The street was lined with well-wishers, not only of the Japanese ethnic group but of many ethnic groups.

Hawaiʻi was home to the men and families, men who had counted the days to come "home." Their roots were not historic ones; their roots were nevertheless deeply embedded in Hawaiʻi.

Home was where one gave and received an unselfish type of love, the men realized, smothered with affection and happiness. Their bodies had been in internment camps, but their spirits had been in the hearts and minds of those they loved and who loved them.

Furuya was at peace. Would Kazuo Sakamaki, Pacific War Prisoner #1, also find peace when he returned to Japan? Would friends and relatives who loved him welcome him as a human being and not as someone who had brought or not brought honor to his country?

"Sakamaki-san, keep alive that spirit of yours! We Hawai'i people loved and respected you as a person. We are calabash cousins!"

The Mainlanders, the Panamanians and Peruvians.

"Calabash cousins! Yes, let's treat others as calabash cousins!"

Now it was homecoming time! Furuya smiled and waved "Aloha! Aloha!" as he stepped off the gangplank.

"Aloha! Aloha! the crowd roared back, many with tears streaming uncontrollably.

Furuya spotted his wife, sons, and daughter.

He hurried to his family waiting shyly for him.

{ 4 }

George Ariyoshi

Father and Mother: Otagai and Seeing the Bright Side

Born in 1926, George Ariyoshi was the youngest of the Democrats who took over the legislature of the territory of Hawaii in 1954.

Twenty years later he became the first of Japanese ancestry and the first non-white governor in the United States. He served for more than 13 years. At the age of 59, he finished his last year as governor.

Throughout his political career, Ariyoshi would say that he was influenced greatly by his mother's perpetual sense of optimism and father's philosophy of human relations.

In his talks about his own view of leadership and working with others, Ariyoshi would often cite the principle of *otagai*. He would say that his father taught him that *otagai* means a deep sense of mutual obligation to others no matter how small or little someone's actions might be:

> "As governor, I wanted every person to be willing to listen to the other person's point of view, not necessarily for the purpose of going along, but to be attuned to a wide range of thought and opinion. If we put all viewpoints on the table, we can learn from them. I was reminded almost daily that some people are vocal, but

49

others are not. You always hear from the people who are loud and speak up. Because of this, political leaders have a responsibility to draw out the views and feelings of the people who are less vocal. This occurs when the principle of *otagai* is practiced, when mutuality is understood and mutual respect is exercised."

The difference between failure and success is not that great. People have similar talents but they have differences in performance. We see this in athletics, when one team is better on some days, and another team is better on others. It's that little bit of difference, that little bit of effort, doing the right things, doing them in the right way, recognizing that you have other people who are involved, trying to be fair, trying to do your best under any circumstances, and knowing it is not only the big things but the little things that count."

Governor Ariyoshi talking with people in a small group, 1978.

We are fortunate that Ariyoshi provides for us here precious memories of his life as a child of an Issei father and mother and the traditional principles he never deserted.

Father and Mother: Otagai and Seeing the Bright Side

My father was lean and muscular, and he was known in his younger days for his skill as a *sumo* wrestler. When I was a boy I always saw him as strong and self-assured. He guided me with a sense of confidence and certainty. When I grew up I was amazed to learn how difficult his life had been. He was born in a small village in the prefecture of Fukuoka, Japan. Although he was an excellent student, he only went to school through the third grade. When he was young he went to sea. When he arrived in Hawaii he liked what he saw and jumped ship. As a result, he struggled not only with being an immigrant who spoke little English, but also with being an illegal alien. During World War II, he lived with the expectation that he would be interned.

In the ancient sport of *sumo*, wrestlers are given special names. His *sumo* name was "Yahata Yama," and for many years he was known casually by this name, and not Ariyoshi. The first year I was to campaign, which was thirty-five years after his arrival in Hawaii, I was surprised to hear people greet him as "Yahata."

We moved a lot, but I remember best our two-room place at the corner of Smith and Pauahi streets in Chinatown, just above Honolulu harbor. One of those rooms was a dining room, living room, and a bedroom as well. In Japanese style the dining table was low and we sat on mats on the floor while we ate. At bedtime, the table was rolled away and our *futon* bedding was unrolled onto the mat floor.

Papa often worked on the waterfront as a stevedore. He also got work as a stone mason, but he had an entrepreneurial streak. He contracted to supply gravel to road builders, and he quarried the rock, which required the blasting of dynamite. He didn't want to ask anybody else to do it, so he learned to blast the dynamite himself. He also made *tofu* and sold it, and he eventually opened a dry-cleaning shop in lower Kalihi. He was also to become a campaigner with seemingly boundless reserves of energy.

Nobody in politics knew my father before 1954 when I first ran for elective office. But during the campaign my father was all over the place. He spoke little English. "My boy, my son," was often about the limit of what people understood from him.

My father worked hard every day going door to door. My mother was really active in the campaign too. They would go out in the morning and distribute brochures and put up posters and in the evening, meet me at rallies, which then were held also nightly. Jean, my wife to be, was already campaigning too, tacking up posters around rural Oahu.

My mother was from Kumamoto Prefecture, which is next to Fukuoka in southwestern Japan. Like my father she had only an elementary-school education. Also like my father, she had an amazing way of seeing the bright side of things when she might have despaired. Because our family shared a communal kitchen, she usually got up at four-thirty to start the day's cooking. When she cooked our favorite dishes, she would announce she wasn't hungry. In fact she said she did not care for a particular dish, and she would pass her share on to us. At the time I thought it strange that she did not care for such delicious food, and it was not until long afterward that I saw through her little story.

My parents' idea of opportunity was the opportunity to work hard, be free to improve their lot in life, and raise a family. I was born in 1926, the first of six children. I had one brother and four sisters. Although our two rooms were on the second floor of a rough-board building, I never thought of our place as a tenement, nor did I think of ourselves as poor.

We had a positive sense of our neighborhood, our schools, and of Hawai itself. Family life sheltered us, and within this nurturing environment we practiced discipline willingly and happily. We were free to venture out, but I adhered to the boundaries set by my parents. My mother wanted to know what I was doing, so I always told her, "*Okaasan,* I'm going to such-and-such a place." If I was going to some other place afterward, I would go back and tell her where I would be next, so she always knew where I was. From that point of view, I was quite protected. We were a tightly knit family, and my parents were totally in control, yet I didn't feel I was being deprived of freedom.

I was constantly told there was a right path, and there was no question that I was to follow it. My father was always saying to me, "Do the things that are right. Never mind what happens." In the terms of my Japanese ancestry, it was my obligation to avoid bringing shame. *Haji*—not to bring shame to family and friends—to be honorable always.

His beliefs were derived from a code that was both an inner code and a community code. The two ran together so harmoniously as to be almost one and the same. What you knew to be right came from within, yet it was intertwined with the individual doing right in the eyes of others. He used the Japanese word *otagai*, referring to the deep Japanese sense of mutual obligation. He used the words *okage sama de*, an expression of appreciation for the support and assistance of others, which is sometimes translated as, "I am what I am because of you."

He would say, "Remember to be considerate of other people. Be grateful that you can get help from other people. Acknowledge others. Be humble, because many other people help make things possible for you."

The essence of my father's thinking accompanied me through my career and into the governorship. In my role as governor, I began using some of the Japanese words my father had used to explain my

Mother and father as they appeared when I was reaching adulthood.

Our two-room place at Smith and Pauahi streets, in downtown Honolulu.

beliefs. *Okage sama de*, because of your shadow which falls on me, because of your help, because of you, I am what I am. I reminded myself of that idea often, and I tried to nurture that attitude in others. We are extensions of one another, and we are beholden to one another.

In 1971, a few days after my forty-fifth birthday, my father said to me in Japanese, "Oh, you've become a man now." It is kind of odd to hear that translated into English, but I knew it was a pronouncement of his confidence in me. He used the words "*ichinin mai ni natta*," meaning I had become a full person, that I had reached my potential and had become an adult in a real sense. He said I would continue to grow, that I had a great deal more to learn and do and accomplish, but he was satisfied. My father was also saying he was convinced that the next time around I was going to become governor.

My birthday is on March 12, and I think we had our conversation shortly after that, on March 14. He usually did not go to Japan until around June, but that year he went right after our conversation, because his brother was having his sixtieth birthday party and wanted him there. Papa caught a cold. It got much worse, and he was put in Kumamoto University Hospital. My mother called me to come see him. When I got there the doctor told me it was too bad I had come so far. He wanted me to understand my father would probably not know I had come.

When I went in there, my mother told my father that I had come. I bent over and said, "Papa, can you hear me?" He gasped and said yes, *hai*. He put his arms up and put his hands around my neck, and he pulled me toward him.

The doctor was watching. He said, "You must be very close to your father. If I had not seen it I would not have believed he could do that."

A trade mission from Hawaii was headed for Tokyo. The governor was to have headed it but could not, so he had asked me to do so. I told my mother I was going to cancel my involvement with the trade mission, but she insisted that I not. She said, "You're not a private person now. You're a public person. I understand that, and Papa understands that, and if he felt that because of his condition he kept you from discharging your public responsibilities, he would feel terrible. You've got to go." I went to Tokyo to meet the group as they came into the airport, and I was with them for the business meetings. Then my mother called me to tell me that my father was not doing well at all. I couldn't get a flight out, so I took the train. A distant relative met me at the station and told me that my father had passed on. Later he said when he saw the reaction on my face he felt terrible, and that he never wanted such a responsibility again. When I saw my mother in Kumamoto, I started to say, "I shouldn't have gone," but she stopped me. "Don't say that. You did the right thing," she said.

We brought my father's body back to Hawaii and held his funeral services here. When he first had seen Hawaii he had said, "This is nice, I think I'll stay," and his life turned out to be an amazing saga.

In 1974 I was elected Governor and served until 1986. My mother would always watch for the light to be on in my study, or at the Capitol. If it was on, she knew I was working, and she would stay awake out of lifelong habit. A buzzer connected her room at Washington Place to ours, and one morning the buzzer rang about six-thirty. Jeannie and I found my mother lying on the floor, very pale. She had fallen. She moved only with great difficulty. When I asked her when this happened, she said it was about five-thirty.

I told her, "That was an hour ago. Why didn't you buzz us earlier?"

She said, "You were working until early this morning, and you needed your rest."

When we took her to the hospital, we found she had fractured her pelvis and both legs. Her fall permanently limited her mobility, but she nonetheless remained positive and cheerful. Her hands were always moving, doing things for others. She took great pleasure in making things and giving them away. Whether it was pin cushions or pot holders, artificial flowers or a cover for a tissue box, she made things by the hundreds.

Whenever she met somebody, or somebody came over, she would have a gift for them that she had made herself. She bought yarn in huge boxes. One night, she was trying to transform her huge box of yarn into rolls, and it was getting tangled as it came out. I sat and held the yarn while she rolled it. I listened to her talk, as I had when I was a child. As I listened, I marveled at her persistent good cheer in the face of such discomfort.

The cultural traditions my mother knew best were the traditions of early twentieth-century Japan. She was one of the many first-generation immigrants who came to Hawaii and perpetuated the cultural practices of the old country. As a result, if we went out on New Year's Eve, we would be home before midnight. Bamboo and pine decorated the doorways (as they do still). We ate *soba* noodles and popped firecrackers on the stroke of twelve. Then we would bathe, dress in new clothes, and at two-thirty in the morning we would go to the Koto Hiro Jinsha temple in Palama and say a prayer for the New Year. In these practices, and many more, my mother was traditionally Japanese. She did not speak much English—she could understand a little, but not very much—and she had difficulty conversing with somebody unless they spoke Japanese.

When Emperor Hirohito and his wife visited Hawaii, my favorite photograph from that much-photographed event was my mother graciously bowing to the emperor. It reflects the special feeling of the first-generation immigrants for the emperor of Japan. For one of the emperor's public appearances, I had a section of seats set aside for people 85 and older. Their arrival time was to be around six p.m., but at three o'clock I was notified that many were already seated—and in the hot sun of mid-afternoon. I sent a message that those seats were reserved for them, and to please get out of the sun, but they continued to sit and wait. When our party arrived, I suggested that the emperor greet them. This entailed a walk of about fifty yards. As the day had gone on, the State Department representative had become increasingly officious, and he flatly said no, the emperor would not greet these people who had waited so long. I leaned over to the State Department man and said, "This is Hawaii, and I am taking charge now." As the emperor approached the group, every head went into a deep bow. I saw tears coming down many of the people's cheeks, and I am sure the emperor saw this too.

My mother from the time I was little never scolded me for doing anything wrong. Instead she told me what was right. I always knew that when I needed support, she would be there. She never saw bad or evil in people, not only with us children, but with everyone. She always looked for the silver lining, and she moved us to look in that direction as well. She started each new day by praying. "Thank you God for…" and she would recite the names of each member of the family, and then recite the names of friends. Even in her most senior years, when she was in a wheelchair, she continued to go to the Senior Citizen's Center. She would listen to the complaints of the elderly people and say, "Oh, but you had some good times too. You had pleasant moments, didn't you?"

After we left Washington Place, Jeannie continued to take personal care of my mother, which was not easy, because my mother was bedridden. She was diabetic, and her foot had to be amputated. Finally mother needed intensive care to the point where we had to move her to a nursing home, and then to a hospital. The doctor told us she could be kept alive only by putting her on life-support machines, and that she would not be able to converse or even recognize us—she would be inert and unknowing. He asked us to think together and let him know what we wanted him to do. My brother and sisters and I got together. I said *okaasan* had had a good life. She had given us so much, and it would be asking too much of her to just keep her alive in an unfeeling state, just because we couldn't let go. We all decided that if need be we had to let go as an expression of our love and respect for her. I told the doctor to make her comfortable, but not to do anything to prolong her life. Within fifteen min-

Governor Ariyoshi's mother greets Emperor Hirohito at Washington Place
along with Ariyoshi's sons, Ryozo and Donn.

utes she was gone. It was as though she wanted us to tell her it was
all right.

When my mother passed away, the kids got together and we
talked. I told them that when I was little, I thought our mother was
funny, because the things that I enjoyed eating, the delicious, the
tasty, *ono* things, mother didn't care for. She would say, "You folks go
ahead and eat." I said she saw light even in darkness, and she saw the
goodness in every person.

Mama was 91 years old when she died. Our daughter Lynn
had been trying to conceive a child for some time, and right around
the time of mother's death she became pregnant with her son Sky.
We cannot help but feel their souls are intertwined—that our grandson is mama's gift to us.

Fumiko Kaya

The Legacy of Katsu Goto: Helping Others

Katsu Goto was one of the first Japanese immigrants to work on a sugar plantation in the 1880's. He was lynched in 1889. When Fumiko Kaya, the niece of Katsu Goto, first visited his grave in Honokaa in 1965, she found the grave stone broken and the site untended. She asked for help, and the local Japanese American community raised the necessary funding, not only to restore the gravesite, but to build a memorial in his honor. Fumiko Kaya spent the rest of her life dedicated to the memory of her uncle. It was her hope that greater understanding between the people of Japan and the United States would prevent such a tragedy from happening again.

The following story is adapted from Taron Murakami's honors thesis on Katsu Goto, and is based primarily on Murakami's interviews with Fumiko Kaya. Murakami, a University of Hawaii Regents Scholar, tells us that Goto was an individual man who, despite the hardship of plantation labor, saw the potential for creating a new life in Hawaii for himself and his fellow Japanese immigrants. This is a story that deserves more than passing mention in Hawaii's history.

The Legacy of Katsu Goto: Helping Others

Katsu Goto was born in 1862 in Terasaka Kokufu Village in Kanagawa prefecture, Japan. Katsu was an exceptional student with a global mindset; he excelled in English and was one of the first laborers to travel to Hawaii as a government-contract migrant on the *City of Tokio* in 1885. Nine hundred forty-three men, women, and children were on that ship, and they were the first wave of Japanese immigrants following the arrival of the Gannenmono in 1868.

Goto worked on a three-year contract for the Ookala Sugar Company on the Hamakua Coast of the Big Island. He was allocated lodging, medical care, and wages of $9 per month. Though working and living conditions were difficult, Goto managed to save enough money to send his brother to business school in San Francisco. At the end of his three-year contract, Goto moved off the plantation and opened a store in Honokaa. He was one of the earliest of the Japanese immigrants to open his own business.

Goto's ability to open a store came as result of his relationship with other Japanese immigrants. When his friend, Bunichiro Onome, a Japanese immigration official, decided to return to Japan, he transferred his store permit to Goto. Goto also received financial assistance from a *tanomoshi*, a lending group made up of community members. With help from his friends, Goto began his life as a storekeeper in a one-story building on what is now Mamane Street in Honokaa.

Goto proved to be a savvy businessman, selling goods from Honolulu for lower prices than other stores, and allowing his customers to pay on credit. He also sold specialty items like Japanese medicines that provided comfort to the Japanese laborers who were far from home. His customers were of many ethnicities, but Japanese workers especially patronized the store because Goto had once been a laborer himself. The Japanese community grew around his store; due to his standing as a former laborer and current businessman, as well as his facility with English, many of the Japanese laborers would come to him for advice. Goto served as interpreter and liaison between the workers and management, and helped them advocate for fairer conditions. However, Goto's success, as both businessman and community leader, did not endear him to the Caucasian elites in the area.

Tensions came to a head when one of the plantation fields was set on fire. The plantation owner, Robert M. Overend, suspected Goto had encouraged the Japanese laborers to set the fire in retaliation for poor working conditions. Though officials identified and arrested another suspect, Overend was not satisfied. Tensions continued and the laborers sought Goto's advice. On the night of October 28, 1889, Goto went to talk to some of the Japanese laborers on the Overend camp. After dark, he left on horseback to return to Honokaa. It was the last time the Japanese workers would see him alive.

Goto's body was found the next morning hanging from a telephone pole. The October 31, 1889 Daily Pacific Commercial Advertiser describes the scene and notes: "A new two-inch rope, evidently purchased for the purpose, was used, and from all appearances no bungling hands performed that work—the dead man's hands and legs were pinioned and a genuine hangman's knot under his left ear. No particulars are known yet."

Sheriff Edward G. Hitchcock led the investigation into Goto's murder. Prior to his appointment as sheriff, Hitchcock had worked as manager of Hitchcock & Co.'s Sugar Plantation, so had personal experience working with plantation laborers. To Hitchcock, it was clear early on that the murder had not been committed by another Japanese or Chinese laborer. He took special care to ensure the investigation was carried out in a thorough manner. In addition, the Japanese government hired Keigoro Katsura, a Japanese lawyer working in the United States, to work on the case. Officials in both Japan and Hawaii were concerned that the murder would strain relations between the two countries. Katsura and Hitchcock both worked conscientiously to create the conditions for a fair trial. Katsura's investigation determined that the knots of the rope used to hang Goto were tied neither the Hawaiian or Japanese way, which led the way for the initial arrests. However, despite Hitchcock's and Katsura's efforts, the sentences were light. Instead of murder, four suspects were found guilty of manslaughter. Of these suspects, only one served his full sentence. Robert Overend was never arrested, even though Hitchcock suspected he had orchestrated the murder.

Though Katsu Goto's life ultimately ends in violence, his is still a story to be honored. As one of the first Issei immigrants, he set an example by moving beyond plantation life, starting his own business, and serving as a resource for his fellow Japanese laborers. Goto's story is commendable, not just because he was one of the first Issei to become financially self-sufficient and successful, but because he then committed himself to helping and leading others, even at the risk of his own safety. In the generations that succeeded Katsu Goto, in the successful Japanese American communities that emerged in Hawaii, his legacy will live on.

Katsu Goto's grave and memorial are still in Honokaa. Visitors are welcome to pay tribute to him. Honokaa is located on the northeastern coast of the Big Island, about 55 miles north of Hilo and between the towns of Kamuela and Laupahoehoe, and can be reached by traveling north on Route 19 from either Hilo or Kona. A familiar landmark on the main highway is Tex Drive-In. The site of Katsu Goto's store, the Goto Memorial, and the telephone pole where he was hung is on Route 240, also called Mamane Street, the main road through Honokaa. The three are across the street from

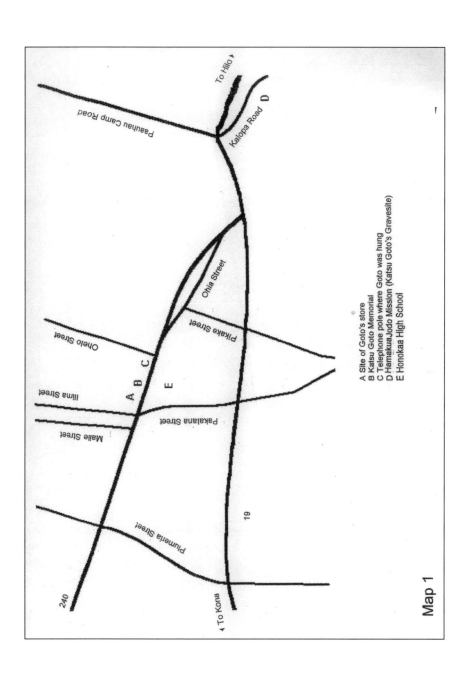

A Site of Goto's store
B Katsu Goto Memorial
C Telephone pole where Goto was hung
D Hamakua Jodo Mission (Katsu Goto's Gravesite)
E Honokaa High School

Map 1

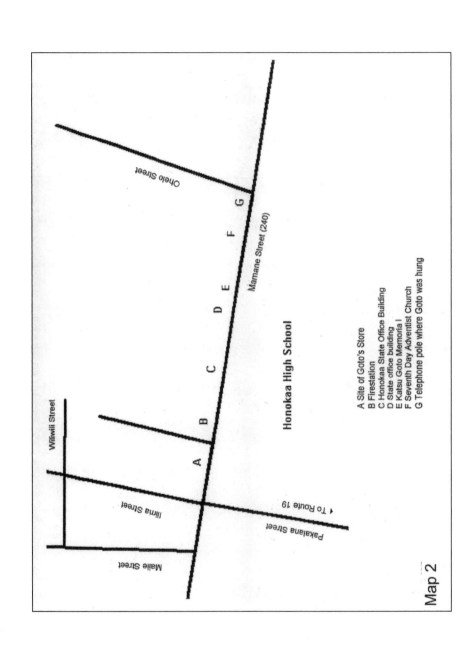

Willilwili Street

Ohelo Street

Iilima Street

Malle Street

Pakalana Street

◄ To Route 19

Mamane Street (240)

A B C D E F G

Honokaa High School

A Site of Goto's Store
B Firestation
C Honokaa State Office Building
D State office building
E Katsu Goto Memoria l
F Seventh Day Adventist Church
G Telephone pole where Goto was hung

Map 2

The only known photo of Katsu Goto,
kept at the Hamakua Jodo Mission.

Two pillars hold up a roof and plaque with a dedication to Goto written in both English and Japanese. The roof is made of 400 clay tiles and the pillars are of ohia wood and a special piece of Hinoki wood from Hiroshima. At the base of each pillar is a symbolic stone. At the base of the right pillar is a stone from Waipio Valley; on the left is a cut of granite from Hiroshima. The memorial symbolizes the strong connection between Hawaii and Japan.

Katsu Goto's grave at the Hamakua Jodo Mission.
It is regularly cared for by Masateru and
Violet Oketani.

Fumiko Kaya and Taron Murakami

Honokaa High School. Katsu Goto's grave is located at the Hamakua Jodo Mission (Paauhau). To visit, drive up Kalopa Road (across from Paauhau Camp Road) which is on the mauka side of the highway. There will be a sign for "Hamakua Jodo Mission" on the mauka side of the road. Fumiko Kaya would be happy to know that people still visit and remember her uncle.

{ 6 }

Fujio Matsuda

Human and Family Values Unite Us

Fujio Matsuda was the ninth President of the University of Hawaii. He was the first Asian American to be appointed president of a major university in the United States. He served from 1974 to 1984.

Matsuda was born and raised in Kaka'ako, a community of immigrants from many Pacific, Asian, and American ethnic cultures. His father, Yoshio, came to Hawaii in 1919. After working on a sugar plantation on Kauai, he moved to Honolulu where he met and married Shino Iwasaki.

A soft-spoken individual of few words, Fujio Matsuda shares with us what he learned from his mother, and from his experiences growing up in Hawaii and on the mainland.

Human and Family Values Unite Us

My mother was the fifth daughter in a family of nine children and had only a sixth-grade education. With my father, she started a Chinese noodle restaurant in Kaka'ako, which became very successful. A recipe learned from a Chinese cook was modified by my mother by adding Japanese soup stock ingredients proved a huge success. The

71

saimin noodles and *wonton* (meat filled dumplings) were Chinese, and the *udon* noodles were Japanese. Meat sticks marinated in Japanese soy sauce and broiled over charcoal fire completed the menu.

It was a family business, so everyone helped. My three sisters helped out while going to school and, later, while working full-time at their day jobs. They helped to prepare the ingredients and to cook and serve the noodles after school or work. My father preferred to work in the background, making the noodles and *wonton* during the day, broiling the meat sticks and washing the dishes. When I was old enough, I helped with the *saimin*-making part. My mother was the "general manager." She did the procurement of all the supplies, paid bills and tended to the customers when my sisters were not available. People called our restaurant Matsuda Saimin or Kaka'ako Saimin Stand. At its peak, a bowl of saimin was about 25 cents and barbeque meat stick, 10 cents. We really had steady customers so my mom made a lot of friends from all over Honolulu. We closed Sundays. One day a week. Saturday was the busiest day. My mom would work 15 to 18 hours a day.

Growing up in Kaka'ako, my mother spoke to me basically in Japanese. But what she taught me went beyond just being Japanese. She taught me that at the human level, person to person level, people are all the same. They all share the same values. Things like race, color, religion, geography, history, language, and customs identify and differentiate people but human and family values unite us all.

In the way she lived in her daily life and worked serving her customers who were a mix of people—native Hawaiians, Portuguese, Japanese immigrants and others, she taught me the importance of consideration to all (*omoiyari*), honesty (*shōjiki*), compassion (*nasake*), gratitude (*kansha*), and other fundamental values we all share as human beings.

My world expanded when I entered Pohukaina, a neighborhood public elementary school. The children of other immigrants—Portuguese, Chinese, Filipino, a few Caucasians—and, of course, native Hawaiians, were my classmates. Pidgin English, a mixture of mostly English and Hawaiian words, with some Chinese, Portuguese and Japanese thrown in, served as our medium of communication. We loved Pidgin, while "proper English" was an affectation for classroom use. English was a foreign language that we acquired painstakingly, word by word, following strict rules.

My cultural transition, however, was not directly from Japanese to American. I felt strongly related to the Hawaiian culture. Japanese and Hawaiian culture both share strong family traditions and value heart-to-heart ties among people. Till this day, I love the song, "Mai Poina 'Oe Ia'u." It sounds so beautiful, in a way that only Hawaiians can sing that song. I surprise myself when I find myself singing along.

> Mai poina 'oe ia'u
> (Do not forget me)
> E ka'u mea e li'a nei
> (Beloved, of my heart)
> E ho'omaumau ka 'ikena
> (Let your visits be more frequent)
> I mau ai ke ko'i'i a loko
> (That the invigorating love remains, within)

Pearl Harbor, December 7th, 1941 changed my world. I was a senior in McKinley High School, class of 1942. I joined the 442nd Regimental Combat Team in March 1943, one of 2000 all Hawaii Japanese volunteers. Toward the end of our basic training in Mississippi, I was ordered by the army to receive special training in Alabama, and then assigned to the 291st FAOB (Field Artillery Observation Battalion) where I joined young men from all over the country, a cross section of white, young America. I was the only Asian. Inevitably, I am asked, was I subjected to racial discrimination in the army? My answer is, "Not to my knowledge." Curiosity, yes, for I was an oddity. Most of them had never known a Japanese American. On the other hand, my comrades who came from all over white America were an oddity to me, as well.

The only white Americans I knew in Hawaii were my teachers; I had no *haole* friends. In the segregated army of World War II, we had no blacks. I guess I was technically "not black," which put me in a white army unit. As I look back, it was my Japanese and Hawaiian multi-cultural upbringing that put me at ease among my new all-white comrades.

We went overseas together and fought the war in Northern Europe. I experienced in my life even more that we were all different but shared the same aspirations and values. Race, color, religion, geography, history, language, customs, etc. identified and differentiated groups, but human and family values united us.

My white comrades and I became lifelong friends. At that time, I was made a squad leader and I became especially close to Bailey Merrill who was our platoon commander. He was a lawyer by profession and a teacher by inclination. We became, not just comrades in arms, he was like an older brother I never had. After the war, I resumed my life as a student at the University of Hawaii in familiar, comfortable surroundings. At the end of my sophomore year, I decided to transfer to a mainland college, something unthinkable before the war, but with the G.I. bill to finance my college education and my broadened cultural outlook, it was an easy transition.

Bailey Merrill helped me find a good engineering college, Rose Polytechnic Institute in Terre Haute, Indiana, close to where he lived and practiced law in Evansville. Attesting to the quality of education at Rose Poly, when I applied to graduate school, I was accepted at MIT (Massachusetts Institute of Technology).

In June 1949, I returned to Hawaii to marry Amy Saiki, a McKinley Class of '43 graduate. That was sixty-three years (in 2013) and six children ago. I called Bailey to let him know that I would be stopping in Evansville to introduce my new bride to him and his

Fujio Matsuda and his mother Shino with family and friends
before he leaves on his flight from Honolulu International Airport.

wife Josephine on our way to MIT. He said, "Great! We'll drive you
there." I was sure he misunderstood and started to explain, to which
he said, "I know where MIT is; Jo and I will drive you there." We
always joked about our chaperoned honeymoon to Niagara Falls,
Canada (Toronto, Montreal and Quebec) and down the Maine
coast to Boston.

Bailey later became an Eisenhower Republican in the U.S.
Congress. He once escorted my father and me through the House
chambers and onto the floor, where only members are allowed when
the House of Representatives is in session. What a thrill it was for
an immigrant and his second-generation son. We exchanged visits
many times since, Honolulu and Evansville. Years later, when our
grandson got married in Nashville, with two of our children accom-
panying us, we took that occasion to visit Bailey's and Jo's grave in

Evansville. They had known "Uncle Bailey" and "Aunty Jo," who had never had their own children, but did have six *hānai* Matsuda children. I also named my first son Bailey after him. Yes, we were all family.

After the war, throughout my schooling on the G.I. bill in Indiana and MIT and in my professional career as a Director of the State Department of Transportation (DOT), professor and President of the University of Hawaii, I have met many individuals, some with impressive resumes, power and wealth. But my view of human beings, as my mother taught me in spoken Japanese, growing up in Hawaii and mainland experiences, has remained the same—at the human, person-to-person, and family level, we all share the same values.

Human and family values unite us all. No matter the color of our skin, race, place, language, we are all human beings. Our lives are equal.

Epilogue

"Who you?" is an intriguing question. It is one that invites all of us to learn the stories of who we are. For Japanese Americans of Hawaii, they are the stories of the Issei.

Understanding one's identity is to honor the first generation. We are indebted to Masaji Marumoto, Sparky Matsunaga, Patsy Saiki, George Ariyoshi, Fumiko Kaya, and Fujio Matsuda for the personal reflections they have shared with us. Their stories of the Issei help us to know the meaning of the words "*okage sama de*." "Kage," as George Ariyoshi explains, can be translated as "shadow." In tribute to the Issei, "*okage sama de*" is to say "because of your presence, because of your shadow that falls on me, I am what I am."

The year 2018 marks the 150th anniversary of Japanese in Hawaii. Since the arrival of the Gannenmono, the population spans six generations and totals nearly 300,000 individuals. They are an integral part and contribute greatly to the nature of island society. Cultural elements of Japan, America, and Hawaii, uniquely shared, are the mainstays of their lives.

They do not take for granted a 150 year history. They hear the Issei voice, "Lucky come Hawaii." They say to themselves, "How fortunate I am to call Hawaii home—to have ancestors who chose to work, stay and cast their lot together with the people of Hawaii."

To know "who you" is to know the Issei. On the journey of life, the Japanese Americans of Hawaii do not walk alone. The Issei walk with them. They do not lose their way.

Afterword

The World of the Issei, the 1930's—A Photographic Glimpse

Initially, sugar plantations defined the landscape of the Issei world. But by the 1930's, most Issei had moved off the plantations into Honolulu and other island towns.

With the greater part of their life ahead of them, they found work in many different occupations.

DISTRIBUTION OF JAPANESE BY OCCUPATION—1930

Occupation	Males	Females	Total
Sugar Plantations	6,664	567	7,231
Pineapple	2,511	579	3,090
Rice Cultivation	131	28	159
Coffee Cultivation	828	298	1,126
Vegetable Truck Farming	998	259	1,257
Horticulture	208	60	268
Dairy/Piggeries/Poultry Raising	814	144	958
Various Agriculture	1,331	371	1,702
Domestic Servants	1,285	1,599	2,884
Agricultural Laborers, misc.	1,671	286	1,957

(continued)

80 Afterword

Occupation	Males	Females	Total
Day Laborers	968	125	1,093
Fishing	969	5	974
Laundry Workers	249	371	620
Food Manufacture & Processing	149	58	207
Confectioners and Bakers	39	5	44
Misc. Manufacturing	525	16	541
Tailors/Seamstresses	195	672	867
Construction Contractors/Carpenters/ Masons/Painters/Plumbers	4,416	1	4,417
Auto Repair	461	6	467
Retail/Drugstores/Drygoods/Clothing/ Cooks/Jewelry, misc.	2,139	370	2,509
Electricians/Surveyors/Draftsmen/Engineers	230	—	230
Hotel/Inns/Boarding Houses/Barbers	414	381	795
Restaurants/Pool Houses/Entertainers	247	99	346
Railroad/Auto Drivers/ Freighters	1,665	—	1,665
Artists/Photographers/Musicians	104	8	112
Nurses/Midwives/Masseurs	67	193	260
Reporters/Insurance Salesmen	114	—	114
Buddhist & Shinto Priests	146	7	153
Christian Workers	27	4	31
Office Workers/Bank Clerks, etc.	3,374	479	3,853
Educators	336	455	791
Doctors	60	—	60
Dentist	46	—	46
Pharmacists	35	—	35
Legal/ Attorneys	23	1	24
Government Workers	135	3	138
Others	3,159	575	3,734
Total	36,733	8,025	44,758

Source: Kihara, Ryūkichi. Hawii Nihonjinshi (A History of Japanese in Hawaii). Tokyo: Bensei-sha, 1935.

The 1930's mark a significant period in the lives of the Issei. For many, it was the decade that Issei became an integral part of Hawaii's community. In the business sector, they opened laundries, cotton factories, sake breweries, family restaurants, and bakeries. They started poultry, hog, fish, vegetable, fruit, and flower farms, among other establishments. They became significant members in skilled trades. They were Hawaii's carpenters, plumbers, electricians, mechanics, and contractors.

With the rise of Issei in business, the 1930's also marked the rise of Japanese community institutions. Language schools, religious temples and churches were established. Social, professional and civic organizations formed. Time devoted to leisure activities, sports, and community celebrations became more a part of the Issei's activities and family life.

The Issei were truly becoming a major group in building Hawaii's society. Though the Issei were defined as aliens and could not vote, their American born children were coming of age. In 1920, Japanese constituted less than 3 percent of Hawaii's registered voters. Six years later, they made up nearly 8 percent. But by 1936, 25 percent, one out of four registered voters in Hawaii was of Japanese descent. The children of the Issei were the largest voting group in the islands.

Needless to say, in the 1930's, the burgeoning Issei community laid the foundation for future generations.

The following photos, taken in the 1930's, provide a glimpse of the Issei world and the community they built. The photos are from the *Nippu Jiji,* which was the largest Japanese newspaper at the time. The *Nippu Jiji* maintained an extensive file of thousands of images taken of Issei before World War II. The photos here were made available to us through the auspices of the *Hawaii Times (Nippu Jiji)* Photo Archives Foundation and the Japanese Diaspora Initiative, Hoover Institution, Stanford University.

The curator of Stanford University, Hoover Institution Library

and Archives Hoji Shinbun Digital Collections (https://hojishinbun
.hoover.org), Dr. Kaoru "Kay" Ueda writes that the importance of
the *Nippu Jiji* photos cannot be underestimated. The *Nippu Jiji* was
one of the most essential sources of information for Hawaii's Issei
community. The photos capture historic moments.

Leisure Time Activities and Sports

Whether through fishing, sports, or martial arts, Issei became active
participants in leisure time activities that would characterize their
Japanese community and island lifestyle.

Sept 11, 1936: Harry J. Kurisaki and friends

1930's: Shunyo Gym

May 2, 1939: Sumo Tournament

Honolulu Restaurants

Issei entrepreneurs entered the Honolulu restaurant business catering to a multicultural clientele with a diverse ethnic palate.

August 11, 1939: Light House Chop Suey

Masaichi Kitagawa, Owner
Light House Chop Suey.
(Also pictured above in a white shirt and tie
below the waitress holding a bottle of beer.)

April 4, 1939: Clipper Café

June 15, 1939: Times Grill

Family Stores

Issei families established stores in Honolulu and other towns to serve the diverse needs of the community.

June 18, 1938: Kanda Store Moiliili

February 20, 1939: Akagi Yoshitate Store

September 22, 1939: Crown Jewelers

Japanese Small Businesses

Enterprising Issei with determination to succeed in building small businesses for the long term started factories and companies.

December 16, 1939: Honolulu Sake Brewing Co.

March 31, 1931: Honolulu Laundry Co.

1930's: Sugita Cotton Factory

Community Celebrations

Issei families with their children, the Hawaii born generation, held public celebrations and supported Japanese commemorative events.

1930's: Hilo Parade

February 11, 1935: 50th Anniversary of Japanese in Hawaii

April 21, 1938: Kapaa Hongwanji Parade

The Japanese Language Schools

The Japanese language schools were established to teach the second generation the language of the homeland so as to facilitate intergenerational dialogue, perpetuate the ties with the homeland and to promote deeper Japanese values among the children.

July 17, 1939: Makiki Japanese School

Students of Makiki
Japanese School

1929: Waikiki Japanese School

September 6, 1939: Chuo Gakuin Japanese Central Institute

Appendix

Key Resources on the Issei

Books

Kimura, Yukiko. *Issei: Japanese Immigrants in Hawaii.* Honolulu: The University Press of Hawaii, 1988.

Author's Introduction (edited segment).

My earliest observations and contact with the Issei of Hawaii began in the years 1920–1923 in Yokohama, when, as a college student, I accompanied a secretary in charge of the YWCA's Emigration Department to the docks to see off and give advice to the young women, the so-called picture brides, who were sailing for Hawaii to marry their picture bridegrooms.

In 1930, I went to Hawaii as a delegate from Japan to attend the second Pan Pacific Women's Conference, sponsored by the Pan Pacific Women's Association of Hawaii, an international meeting of women representing the countries of the Pacific area. From mid-August to mid-October of that year, I visited plantation communities to observe the conditions of the Japanese immigrants. On Hawaii, my itinerary, carefully prepared by Mr. Kango Kawasaki, a lawyer and community leader, included overnight stays in the homes of plantation workers and meetings with them, meetings and discussions with language-school teachers, and a visit to the Rev. Shiro

Sokabe's home for children of plantation workers in Honomuu. On Oahu, in addition to plantation communities, I visited other institutions that were involved with the immigrants' lives and met with several pioneer Nisei. My work was greatly facilitated by the help of people like Umematsu Watada of Nuuanu YMCA: Professor Tasuku Harada of the University of Hawaii; Yasutarō Sōga, editor and publisher of the Nippu Jiji; Mrs. Tsuru Kishimoto, the Japanese secretary of the Honolulu YWCA's International Institute; and Mrs. George Castle, then president of the Honolulu YWCA, who made my stay and study of the conditions of the Japanese immigrants possible.

Most of the data were gathered, however, after February 1938, when I joined the staff of the International Institute of the Honolulu YWCA to be in charge of the work among the Japanese, both the Issei and Nisei. In addition, I was assigned to make a series of studies of the problematic aspects of the Japanese community. The first was of Japanese barbershops and their barber-girls. Since there was no precedent for using women as barbers in Japan or in Hawaii, the large community regarded this unconventional practice with disapproval. There were also complaints that the Japanese barbershops were undercutting the prevailing prices. Another study was of Japanese dressmakers, who drew similar criticism; the study revealed that they were using dressmaking students and could thus lower their prices. Through such studies and my continuous association with individuals and families as well as my participant observation both in the Japanese community and the larger community before, during, and after World War II, I gained intimate knowledge and understanding of the Japanese in Hawaii.

...this book concentrates on the Issei's experience as they saw it and from their own points of view, their own stories, including memoirs...

Saiki, Patsy Sumie. *Ganbare! An Example of Japanese Spirit.* Honolulu: Mutual Publishing, 1982.

Author's Introduction.

This is a true story of about 1,500 Hawai'i residents—Japanese aliens and American citizens—who were suddenly stripped of everything, including a name, to become an anonymous number. Bewildered, dumbfounded, they surrendered everything except the clothes on their back as they were incarcerated in flimsy tents behind barbed wire fences. They wondered, as they lived aimlessly day to day, what the future would bring.

The future brought 100 to over 1000 days of internment. It brought an examination of their past life and of their relationship with the country which they called home but which would not accept them because they were Asians. It brought an awakening and new awareness of self priorities. Guarded by MPs with machine guns and trained dogs, they had to call upon whatever physical, mental, spiritual and intellectual strengths and skills they had to continue as rational human beings.

When bitterness and futility seemed to overcome them, they recalled the Japanese spirit of ganbare!—hold on! keep going! persevere!—which their parents and grandparents had shown. And as they hung on, they developed patience, compassion, and a new perspective on life.

The time is World War II (1941–1945). The facts are reconstructed from many interviews, diaries, books and articles written in Japanese and English, sketches and pictures. The internees still alive after forty years had learned to see their four years of interment in perspective, as part of their total lives in the country of their choice.

GANBARE! is a story of a group of people with unique experiences. To tell their story, they immersed their brushes into their own souls and translated the experiences into an example of the Japanese spirit. This is part of the heritage they are leaving us.

Grant, Glen. *Obake: Ghost Stories in Hawaii.* Honolulu: Mutual Publishing, 1994.

Author's Comments (edited segments).

When I arrived in Honolulu in 1970 to attend the University of Hawaii as a graduate student, I had no idea that the Islands were alive with ghosts. After one semester working in Japanese American studies with Dr. Dennis M. Ogawa, I realized that nearly every student in the class had family ghost stories or even personal experiences with the supernatural.

The *issei*, those Japanese who immigrated to Hawaii in the decades immediately prior to and following the turn of the century, seemed especially keen in preserving the ghostly heritage of their homeland. Considering the Japanese penchant for *obake*, or "weird things," it is small wonder, then, that in plantation camps and urban districts throughout Hawaii the shadowy images of Meiji-era Japan should have moved across the ethnic phantasmagoria...

When the Japanese started arriving in the Islands in large numbers as contract laborers in 1885, those *issei* did not only bring their few personal belongings bundled in their wicker baskets and their avid desire for success—they also brought their ghosts that commingled and "intermarried" with indigenous Hawaiian spirits and those of other races. Every camp had its own hauntings, its *inugami* possessions, its *odaisans*, priests or priestesses who performed miracles and cures, its withcraft and fear of *kahunaism*...

My colleagues urged me to publish these island stories.

Digital Collection

Stanford University. Hoover Institution Library and Archives, Japanese Diaspora Initiative, *The Hoji Shinbun* (https://hojishinbun .hoover.org/).

Curator, Kaoru "Kay" Ueda Introduction.
 The Gannenmono (元年者) was the beginning of the journey of the Japanese seeking a new home in Hawaii and helping shape the diversified society Hawaii enjoys today. It is our honor and privilege to be involved with commemorating the one hundred and fiftieth anniversary of the arrival of the Gannenmono in Hawaii. The Hoover Institution Library & Archives at Stanford University are delighted to have the opportunity to work with the Japanese American community in Hawaii to preserve Hawaii's Issei history and make the Nippu Jiji Photo Archives available to the public. We are thrilled to partner with the Hawaii Times Photo Archives Foundation to shed light on life of Issei, their Hawaii-born children, their businesses, schools, religious institutions, and worldviews on current affairs.
 The *Nippu Jiji* was one of the most influential Japanese newspapers in Hawaii. The importance of newspapers to the Nikkei community, particularly predominantly Japanese-speaking Issei, cannot be underestimated. They supplied essential information for living and working in Hawaii and kept the readers up to date on the news in Japan. Perhaps more important, they provided forum of discussion on major issues that had an enormous impact on the future of the Japanese and the Japanese American community: sugar plantation strikes and Japanese-language schools. Issei Yasutaro Soga was an influential opinion leader in the Nikkei community. He purchased the *Yamato Shinbun* (やまと新聞) daily newspaper and later renamed it to the *Nippu Jiji* in 1906.
 Thanks to the anonymous generous donation to create the Jap-

Yamato Shinbunsha (1896–1906)

Nippu Jiji (succeeded by the Hawaii Times) 1906–1985

anese Diaspora Initiative, we have been able to preserve and make many of the prewar Japanese newspapers in Hawaii and the continental United States available to the public at the Hoji Shinbun Digital Collection (https://hojishinbun.hoover.org/). Collaborating with US and Japanese institutions, the collection has grown some sixty titles and more than half a million pages of newspapers. Its search capability makes this collection unique among those of historical Japanese American newspapers. The oldest Japanese newspaper in Hawaii, the *Nihon Shuho* (日本週報) (Japanese Weekly Times) was first issued on September 26, 1892; its historical value was appreciated by 1934 as shown in the February 17 article on the *Nippu Jiji*. The Hoji Shinbun Digital Collection holds the February 6, 1893 issue of the *Nihon Shuho*, providing a historical testimony of an emerging and vibrant Japanese community in Hawaii.

In the next phase of the project we will incorporate the Nippu Jiji Photo Archives, digitized by Densho, in this digital collection, allowing users to search both newspaper articles and photographs. We are partnering with the National Museum of Japanese History to describe the original captions in both English and Japanese. This is an excellent example of American and Japanese institutions working together with the community in Hawaii, a long-standing local tradition. The photographs in this publication were created or collected at *Nippu Jiji* as part of its newspaper publishing business. Some made it to the newspaper articles; others did not. These photographs not only capture historical moments of the Japanese American community in Hawaii but also provide insight into their worldviews at a given time and their interest in world affairs, particularly pertaining to Hawaii and Japan.

Made available to the public at the Hoji Shinbun Digital Collection, these photos will help uncover individual paths and trajectories of the Issei and their families in Hawaii and unpack their dynamic history. We hope to continue to work with the community in Hawaii to preserve the Japanese American history in the twenty-first century and for future generations.